Quarterly Essay

Quarterly Essay is published four times a year by Black Inc., an imprint of Schwartz Books Pty Ltd. Publisher: Morry Schwartz.

ISBN 9781863951074 ISSN 1832-0953

Subscriptions – 1 year print & digital
(4 issues): $79.95 within Australia incl. GST.
Outside Australia $119.95. 2 years print & digital
(8 issues): $149.95 within Australia incl. GST.
1 year digital only: $49.95.

Payment may be made by Mastercard or Visa, or by cheque made out to Schwartz Books. Payment includes postage and handling.

To subscribe, fill out and post the subscription card or form inside this issue, or subscribe online:

quarterlyessay.com
subscribe@blackincbooks.com
Phone: 61 3 9486 0288

Correspondence should be addressed to:

The Editor, Quarterly Essay
Level 1, 221 Drummond Street
Carlton VIC 3053 Australia
Phone: 61 3 9486 0288 / Fax: 61 3 9011 6106
Email: quarterlyessay@blackincbooks.com

Editor: Peter Craven
Management & Advertising: Silvia Kwon
In-house Editor: Chris Feik
Marketing & Publicity: Angela Crocombe
Design: Guy Mirabella

The *Australian Quarterly Essay* is a new journal that aims to present significant contributions to political, intellectual and cultural debate. Each issue will contain a single writer at a length of at least 20,000 words. *The Australian Quarterly Essay* will not be confined to politics but it will be centrally concerned with it. We are not interested in occupying any particular point on the political map and we hope to bring our readership the widest range of political and cultural opinion that is compatible with truth-telling, style and command of the essay form.

As well as the main essay, each issue of *The Australian Quarterly Essay* will be a forum for ongoing debate relating to previous essays. We welcome correspondence, which will be published in subsequent issues.

INTRODUCTION

Robert Manne's "In Denial: The Stolen Generation and the Right", the first essay in the *Quarterly Essay* series, is an attempt to come to terms with the fact that a group of right-wing commentators (centred in the first instance around Manne's old magazine *Quadrant* under the editorship of Paddy McGuinness) has effectively railroaded the national awareness of how large numbers of Aboriginal children were separated from their families in the period between 1910 and 1970. As Manne presents it, this is a story of how a failure of sympathy, a hardening of the imaginative arteries, is abetted at every point by a form of wishful thinking about the past and compounded by a woefully impoverished sense of evidence. It is the story of how a small group of people have been responsible for minimising or confusing the general apprehension of the great pain inflicted on thousands of Aboriginals, no doubt often enough by people of good will.

Inga Clendinnen once described Robert Manne as a writer of "ravishingly cool" analyses but "In Denial" is not simply cool. It exhibits all of Manne's dispassion but it is also a long polemical essay which not only chops up the opinion men of the right like firewood but which does so in sorrow and in anger.

It is a tightly argued case against McGuinness and the *Quadrant* school of stolen generations deniers that is also a terse and brilliant account of how government policies towards the Aborigines blighted the lives of myriads of harried, dispossessed people, who were left bereft in so many cases of that most elementary of things, the bond between mother and child.

Manne is sword-point sharp in tracing the evolution of the policies that held sway, but he never loses sight of the grief-torn faces. Of Aboriginal mothers fleeing the bush at the mere sight of a policeman's helmet, of young girls strapped for trying to touch a family hand through an institutional fence, of a young boy sent to a series of Homes and prisons (in the 1960s) because he pinched a bicycle from a high school. And of how that same boy, after years in prison for petty offences comes to kill first his sister's boyfriend and then himself. No reader of "In Denial" will soon forget what Malcolm made of the biblical text, "if thine eye offend thee".

"In Denial" is an impassioned defence of the vision of sorrow and pity which the *Bringing them home* report bequeathed to the nation, but it's at the same time not an unqualified endorsement of its detail. Manne is adamant that *Bringing them home* had the great virtue of creating an atmosphere of confidence for the victims themselves. Compared to this the flaws of the report are minor flaws indeed.

And he makes short shrift of the "authorities" who opposed the report: Ron Brunton, the anthropologist who has lent his voice to the interests of the mining companies; Colin Macleod, the one-time junior patrol man; and Reginald Marsh, whose theory of Aboriginal removal Manne sees as a myth and a dangerous one.

The gravest judgment this essay offers is of the opinions expressed by Peter Howson, a former Minister for Aboriginal Affairs.

"In Denial" is a demolition job on the historical demolitionists who have attempted to minimise, to effectively deny, the reality of the stolen generations. When Robert Manne was ousted as editor of *Quadrant*, the main objection of the prime mover, the poet Les Murray, was the account of the

Aboriginal question given by Manne and his close associate Raimond Gaita (who articulated the shame/guilt distinction with maximum clarity).

His successor P. P. McGuinness, one-time man of the left and *Sydney Morning Herald* columnist, promised a new line, devoid of sentimentality and offering a "genuine debate". Manne sees McGuinness as the central strategist in the war on the stolen generations and in his account of McGuinness's writings he provides what looks like a devastating critique of his successor's denials.

Robert Manne's central contention is that the deniers of the stolen generations, the nay-sayers of the Right, created an atmosphere of disbelief in the idea that many Aboriginal children had been treated unjustly. "In Denial" is a comprehensive rebuttal of the group of influential columnists that includes Piers Akerman, Frank Devine, Christopher Pearson, Michael Duffy and Andrew Bolt. Indeed "In Denial" begins very topically with an account of Bolt's supposed "exposure" of Lowitja O'Donoghue in late February of this year.

Many people believe that Andrew Bolt's article was a dangerous beat-up. To the small, highly influential group of right-wing columnists—fuelled with the *Quadrant* evidence Manne contests so convincingly—*Bringing them home* was itself a beat-up that appealed to the "moral vanity" of a left-wing intelligentsia who constituted a "moral mafia" and who wanted to decry the legacy of Australian history.

One of the strengths of Robert Manne's "In Denial" is the persuasiveness with which he suggests that John Howard's government (the government which has refused to apologise to the Aborigines) was in fact collusive with the right-wing *Quadrant*-led campaign against the perspectives that derive from *Bringing them home*. This is highlighted by the account Manne gives of the government's defence in the Cubillo–Gunner case (the stolen generations test case) and the way it was conducted by Douglas Meagher QC.

Manne does not deny that any government would have conducted a "robust" defence but he suggests that the Meagher case for the Howard government exceeded normal bounds. In a brilliant forensic move Manne highlights the fact that Meagher saw fit to address a *Quadrant* seminar on the subject of the Aborigines and shows how the speech he gave misconstrued the evidence about the Harold Blair project in 1960s Melbourne. He relates this in turn to Meagher's father, Ray Meagher, the State Minister for Aboriginal affairs.

So much of what Robert Manne uncovers in this essay is in the category of what T .S. Eliot called "things done and done to others harm which once we took for exercise of virtue". He does not want to decry one eminent barrister's dedication to his father's memory. On the contrary, he says that the catalogue of Aboriginal child removal exhibits every moral type from the sadist to the saint. Nothing in this sad and sobering essay is sadder than the words of the universally admired Sister Kate when she writes to one of the Chief Protectors of Aboriginals: she sees the human face of the problem but not the way past it.

Robert Manne says that Paddy McGuinness's campaign to deny the human face of the stolen generations led him—eventually—to publish an atrocity denial in the form of Keith Windschuttle's attack on the supposed "myth" of frontier killings. Manne sees Windschuttle as proffering no real evidence for his views.

Robert Manne's conclusion to "In Denial" is sorrowful and wondering rather than angry and polemical. He invokes the astonishment of so many Australians at the way the most universal of all values, the love between mother and child, was sundered by the taking away of so many Aboriginal children and he says the deliberate campaign against the sobering and shame-inducing nature of this revelation is cognate with the rise of Hansonism and the ambivalence of John Howard's government.

He sees it as a failure to acknowledge the injustice done and a refusal to feel shame. One thing the reader is liable to feel is appal at the quality of the "evidence" some of Manne's antagonists have marshalled.

But this is one of the most hotly debated issues in contemporary Australia and as editor of *Australian Quarterly Essay* I should say that we welcome detailed responses to Robert Manne's essay. One of the advantages of this series is that it allows the essayist room to present the whole truth in a way that short newspaper columns do not. We will publish replies to this essay in subsequent issues.

Peter Craven

Robert Manne

On 23 February 2000 the Melbourne *Herald-Sun* published on its front page an "exclusive" report concerning what was described as a "shock admission" by one of Australia's most respected Aboriginal leaders, Lowitja O'Donoghue. The essence of the supposed admission was captured by the huge headline—"I Wasn't Stolen".

It is well known to the Australian public that Lowitja O'Donoghue was separated from her Aboriginal mother at the age of two. According to the author of the article, Andrew Bolt, she agreed, in the course of an interview, that the word "removed" rather than "stolen" better suited the personal circumstances of her case. Her mother had borne five children while living with her father, an Irish station worker. Lowitja thought it likely that it was not the government but her father who had been responsible for having all five children sent to the South Australian "half-caste" children's mission, the Colebrook Home at Quorn. Lowitja O'Donoghue told Bolt that if her mother had allowed her children to be taken from her this amounted to what she called "uninformed consent". It was clear, even from Bolt's article, that because of her father's cruel action her mother had suffered an unbearable grief throughout her life. Lowitja O'Donoghue told Andrew Bolt that she had not been able to forgive her father for what he had done.

It ought to have been obvious to the editor of the *Herald-Sun* that Bolt's article was a classic example of what is customarily called a journalistic "beat-up". Invented by the historian Peter Read, "stolen generations" is the term that the Aboriginal people have embraced for their collective tragedy—the separation of thousands of children of mixed descent from their mothers and communities. The term covers a wide variety of circumstances—from forcible removal by agents of the state to the relinquishment of children following the application of moral and legal pressure on powerless young Aboriginal women by those who thought they knew what was best. In discussing the phenomenon of Aboriginal child removal in general, Lowitja O'Donoghue, like everyone else, had in the past used the common term, the stolen generations. When describing her own personal circumstances, however, she had been careful to speak, more simply, of her "removal" from her mother and her community. There was nothing either new or surprising in what she tried to explain to Andrew Bolt. Her only error was to have mistaken a journalist–campaigner for a reporter with a concern for discovering the facts.

It was unclear from Bolt's article whether or not Lowitja O'Donoghue had explained to him how she had come to understand the depth of her mother's suffering following the loss of all her children. It is a story Bolt's readers ought to have been told. During the 1960s, some thirty years after Lowitja had been separated from her mother, she was approached by two old Aboriginal people who were sitting outside the supermarket at Coober Pedy. They told her that they could see in her face the face of her mother and that they knew who she was and from where she came. As it turned out, these old Aborigines were Lowitja's uncle and aunty. They were able to tell her that her mother was still alive and where she lived.

It was several weeks before Lowitja was able to travel to Oodnadatta to find her mother. Her uncle and aunty had, however, told Lowitja's mother about their chance encounter with one of her daughters. When Lowitja finally made it to Oodnadatta she discovered that on every day for the past three months her mother had sat by the roadside awaiting her daughter's return. When they met, Lowitja and her mother could not speak to each other. Her mother knew almost no English. Lowitja, of course, had never learnt her native tongue. Nonetheless they were now together, for the last ten years of Lowitja's mother's life.

Lowitja O'Donoghue, who is a woman of scrupulous honesty and great beauty of soul, has devoted many years of her life to the cause of reconciliation. She has sought to help her fellow Australians understand the tragedies that overtook people like herself and her mother because of the racist belief, no doubt held even by her own father, that "part-white" children had to be "rescued" from the primitive, godless and degraded Aboriginal world. She was rewarded for this work by a nasty national debate over the circumstances of her removal, precipitated by what she rightly described as a "simplistic, sensationalist, misleading and mischievous" report.

On the morning Bolt's beat-up appeared in the Herald-Sun, the Prime Minister of Australia, John Howard, seized his opportunity. He told a commercial radio audience in Melbourne that the revelation that Lowitja O'Donoghue was not stolen was a "highly significant" fact, one, he implied, which vindicated his government's famous denial of the existence of the stolen generations and his even more famous refusal to apologise. Howard called on Australians to cease what he called their pointless "navel gazing" over questions of Aboriginal injustice and to move on.

John Howard, on the morning of February 23, was speaking under the shadow of the strange re-emergence of the racist One Nation Party and the anti-Coalition landslides in Western Australia and Queensland. By underlining his disagreement with Kim Beazley and his agreement with the Hanson voters on the question of a national apology to the stolen generations, John Howard had plainly announced his determination to try to cling to power by playing—as his last hand—what Australians call, crudely but not inaccurately, the race card.

Andrew Bolt's article and John Howard's response were not isolated incidents but the most recent moves of a long campaign to change the moral and political balance with regard to the issue of the stolen generations, and indeed with regard to the Aboriginal question as a whole. It is with this campaign that this essay is concerned.

THE LONG ROAD HOME

In October 1994 the Minister for Aboriginal Affairs in the Keating government, Robert Tickner, addressed the Going Home Conference in Darwin. Of the several hundred Aborigines who attended the conference, very many had been removed from their families and communities as children. Already such people thought of themselves as members of the "stolen generations". At this conference Tickner said that as a minister no issue had so haunted him as this one. He announced he would shortly be writing to Michael Lavarch, the Attorney-General, with the suggestion that the Human Rights and Equal Opportunity Commission conduct an investigation into why thousands of Aboriginal children had been separated from their mothers, families and communities during the course of the twentieth century.

Tickner's letter led, in 1995, to an inquiry headed by Sir Ronald Wilson, former High Court judge and President of the Human Rights and Equal Opportunity Commission, and Mick Dodson, its Social Justice Commissioner. Over two years the inquiry took written and oral evidence, across Australia, from 535 Aboriginal witnesses who had experienced separation at first or second hand. The inquiry had the support of all Australian State and Territory governments. The only government which failed to offer significant assistance was the Howard government, elected in March 1996. It declined to assist the Wilson–Dodson inquiry by producing a history of Commonwealth policy regarding Aboriginal child separation in the Northern Territory. It turned down the inquiry's modest request for some additional funds.

The findings of the Wilson–Dodson inquiry were tabled in the Federal Parliament in May 1997. The inquiry reported that in the period from 1910 to 1970 between one in three and one in ten Aboriginal children had been separated—most by force or under duress or at least with undue pressure. It provided a history of the removal policies and practices in each State and the Northern Territory. It concluded that the physical and mental health of the separated children was probably worse and certainly no better than that of the Aboriginal children who had been spared this fate. A large part of the report consisted of extracts from the testimony of the Aboriginal witnesses who appeared before it. Story after story spoke of psychic and cultural dislocation; terrifying loneliness; physical, sexual and moral abuse; and of continuing pain, numbness and trauma experienced after an often bewildering and inexplicable removal from mother, family, community, world.

The inquiry recommended restitution for the separated children in many forms, including monetary compensation, and most importantly, solemn apologies from the churches and governments involved. According to the relevant United Nations Convention, one means by which genocide can be committed is by removal of children with the purpose of destroying, in whole or even in part, the racial or ethnic group to which they belong. The Wilson–Dodson inquiry concluded that before 1970, and arguably even after that date, the Aboriginal child removal policies and practices of the Commonwealth and State governments made them guilty of genocide, the most serious of all crimes.

No inquiry in recent Australian history has had a more overwhelming reception nor, at least in the short term, a more culturally transforming impact. On the day after *Bringing them home* was tabled, the Leader of the Opposition, Kim Beazley, wept openly in the House. Over the next few days Opposition members read stories contained in *Bringing them home* into

Hansard during the adjournment debates. Overwhelmingly, the media in Australia accepted the general findings of the Wilson–Dodson inquiry and acknowledged the gravity of what the report had revealed. Very rapidly the question of Aboriginal child removal moved from the margin to the centre of Australian self-understanding and contemporary political debate.

Many stolen generations memoirs were now published; films produced; plays staged; songs sung. Hundreds of thousands of citizens signed what were called—in a language borrowed from the Aborigines—Sorry Books. A National Sorry Day was established. It soon seemed to many Australians that no historical question was of greater importance than the stolen generations, no moral matter of greater significance to the life of the nation than the apology to the stolen generations. By now the quest for what we have come to call reconciliation between Aboriginal and non-Aboriginal Australians, and the nature of Australia's response to the issue of the stolen generations, had become altogether intertwined.

Not all Australians shared in this mood. Gradually critics of *Bringing them home* emerged. Some of the criticism came from former administrators of Aboriginal affairs; some from former patrol officers; some from conservative journalists; some from right-wing think-tanks and magazines. It was the magazine *Quadrant*, however, under the editorship of Padraic McGuinness, that marshalled the troops and galvanised the disparate voices of opposition to *Bringing them home* into what amounted to a serious and effective political campaign.

FOUR STORIES

The assessment of the arguments of those involved in the anti-stolen generations campaign cannot take place in a vacuum. Without stories, the understanding of child removal in the first seven decades of the twentieth century is in danger of becoming far too abstract and remote. I have chosen four stories which span the decades and the States and which are, for one reason or another, unusually well documented.

i. *Walter*

The first story is set in 1903. At this time Dr Walter Roth, an eminent anthropologist and the son of naturalised Hungarian Jewish refugees who lived in England, was the Northern Protector of Aborigines in Queensland. Roth was a determined and effective opponent of the economic and sexual exploitation of Aborigines, especially of women and children. As such he made many bitter enemies in Queensland. In 1904 Roth was invited to conduct a Royal Commission into the treatment of Aborigines in the northern areas of Western Australia. He produced a humane and powerful report. Roth was also, as it happens, probably the pioneer in Australia of the policy and practice of Aboriginal child removal. In both his monthly and annual reports to the Queensland parliament, Roth routinely listed the names, ages, localities and, to some extent, the life circumstances of the "half-caste" children he arranged to be sent to the north Queensland Aboriginal missions at Mapoon and Yarrabah. In general it is difficult to discover a great deal from the contemporary records about how the Aboriginal children or their families responded to their removal. In one case, however, the human reality comes vividly alive.

On 17 February 1903 Roth sent a typical letter to the police at Townsville. Roth had recently passed through the township of Cardwell and his attention had been drawn to six "half-caste" children "roaming about the blacks' camp". "I would be grateful", Roth wrote, "by your kindly causing inquiries to be made."

One of the children of interest to Dr Roth was a boy called Walter, aged about fourteen, whose mother, Nellie Bliss, was a full-blood Aborigine. "It seems to me", Roth wrote, "a great pity to see the lad Walter loafing around the camps instead of learning a trade at the Industrial School." Inquiries were duly made. On 8 June Roth recommended that Walter be brought to court and charged, under the Industrial Schools Act of 1865, with being "a child born of an Aboriginal or half-caste mother". Walter was charged with this offence at Cardwell on 18 August 1903. He was sentenced to two years at an industrial school.

On the afternoon following the sentence a telegram was sent by the shire clerk in Cardwell, William Craig, to the Queensland Home Secretary in Brisbane. It read: "Mother half-caste boy Walter weeping outside lock-up says she will kill herself by inflicting blood-letting gashes and starving herself if son taken. May I acting on her behalf pray you to instruct police to return boy pending further inquiry." Craig followed his telegram with a letter. "It is an unassailable and incontestable fact", he wrote after listening carefully to what Nellie Bliss had explained to him, "that Aboriginals treat all children they come in contact with or nurse—half-caste or full-blooded or white—with universal kindness." Nellie Bliss had reared Walter as her people had reared children for centuries. Was this to be regarded as neglect? Was she now to "suffer the mental agony of separation"?

The official in Brisbane who received Craig's letter scrawled across it, "I am not impressed." Nonetheless he asked for further information on the case. The information soon arrived. When Walter was imprisoned he had been sobbing in his cell, while his mother howled and lamented in the street outside. Walter had fallen ill. The wife of the police sergeant at Cardwell feared for his life. Nellie was allowed inside the cell. She nursed Walter back to health. Eventually both were released. Mother and son went to a tracker's hut awaiting news of their fate.

In mid-November Dr Roth reached Cardwell. He took the case of Walter in hand. New warrants were issued. Roth induced William Craig to convince Walter to come on board a steamship, merely, he promised, as a matter of legal formality. Roth pledged to Craig that Walter would then be freed. Instead the boy was seized. Walter tried to jump ship. The native troopers held him down. Walter had not even been able to farewell his mother. He was despatched to the mission at Yarrabah.

Craig was very bitter that he had been persuaded by the police to use his influence to prevent Walter from escaping to the mountains with his Aboriginal stepfather. Walter's stepfather had not for one minute trusted the word of the Queensland government. "The government too much tell im lie, he all day want to stealim blackfellow piccaninny." As it turned out, Craig reflected ruefully, "the old blackfellow knew the character of government officials better than I did."

One of the more insidious racial prejudices of the protectors and police involved in Aboriginal child removal was the conviction, as one put it, that Aboriginal mothers, despite "momentary grief, soon forget their offspring". Nellie Bliss did not forget Walter. On the morning of 18 July 1904 she paid William Craig a visit. She begged his help: "Master you write im letter longa government and tell im me too much cross [sorrowful] me cry all day longa my boy, you tell him quick fellow send im, longa me, me too much poor fellow."

William Craig wrote that evening to the Home Secretary: "The sight of this helpless old gin with tears in her eyes on one side, pleading for her child, and the powerful Queensland government or its officials acting as a kidnapper on the other, has induced me to take up my pen again." Craig told the Home Secretary he had recently met an Aboriginal escapee from Yarrabah who was hiding in the scrub, trying to get back to his land. This man had told him that the blacks at Yarrabah lived in a state of permanent hunger and that Walter, for stealing a piece of bread, had been placed in solitary confinement. Craig pleaded for the Home Secretary's mercy. Would he not allow Walter to go home?

The Home Secretary forwarded Craig's letter to Roth. He responded formulaically. Craig was now beside himself with rage. "I am sorry that the Home Secretary should have thought fit to have forwarded the mother's prayer for mercy to you; the lamb does not expect mercy from the wolf." "Do you dare", he continued, "assert that under English law you have a better right to this boy than the mother who reared and fed him?" William Craig's letter was passed back to the Home Secretary. He advised that no reply need be sent.

In 1906 Walter Roth quit Queensland for British Guiana, worn out by the political opposition that had followed him through his time as Chief Protector of Aborigines. For his part Walter stayed on at Yarrabah. Removal to Yarrabah was for most of its inmates a sentence for life. There is a faded typed page in a file in the Queensland State Archives recording the marriage on 13 April 1910 of a young man now called Walter Cardwell to another "half-caste", Rosie Murray, who had, as it happens, been removed by Dr Roth from the blacks' camp in Maytown in 1902.

ii. *Margaret Tucker*

During the decade after Walter was despatched to Yarrabah, the Aboriginal Protection Board in New South Wales fought a long political battle to have similar powers to those available to Dr Roth—to remove Aboriginal children from their parents—transferred to itself.

By the second decade of the twentieth century an estimated 7,000 Aborigines lived in New South Wales. Fewer than 2,000 were "full bloods"; the remainder were so-called "half-castes"—Aborigines of mixed descent. While the number of "full bloods" was declining, the number of "half-castes" was on the rise. Many Aborigines in New South Wales lived on the stations and reserves. Members of the Board believed that unless something drastic was done—to separate the children from their parents and families—the children would grow up on the settlements to a life of vice and indolence, becoming a permanent financial burden on the state. In its Annual Report to parliament of 1912 the Board expressed its thinking on the nature of the Aboriginal problem in the following words:

> The day is long past when it was possible to segregate the Aborigines. So far as full-bloods are concerned, the Board has done much with the limited funds at their disposal, to make their lot as easy as possible by providing suitable dwellings and supplying them with rations, clothing and blankets, and it is not proposed to interfere with them; but by far the greater number of those the Board have to deal with are half-castes, and others with a lesser degree of Aboriginal blood. With regard to the

adults, it would be obviously harsh to turn a number of those who have families dependent upon them, and who have for years been taught to look upon themselves as Aborigines, away from the Reserves. On the other hand, unless some prompt measures are taken, the children who are now growing up, will, in a few years, be in the same position as their parents. Of these children, a number who are half-castes, quadroons and octoroons, are increasing with alarming rapidity. To allow these children to remain on the Reserves, to grow up in comparative idleness, and in the midst of more or less vicious surroundings would be, to say the least, an injustice to the children themselves, and a positive menace to the State. The only solution of the problem, therefore, is to deal effectively with the children; and, while not unduly interfering with the relationship between parent and child, to see that they are properly trained to spheres of future usefulness, and once away from the Reserves not to allow them to return—except, perhaps, in the case of those who have parents, on an occasional visit. Past experience has shown that the children cannot be properly trained under their present environments, and it is essential that they should be removed at as early an age as possible to ensure success.

At the time this was written all children in New South Wales, including Aboriginal children, could be removed from their parents if neglect could be proved before a court. The problem facing the Board was that most of the Aboriginal children it had its eyes on were not suffering neglect. As the Board explained to the Chief Secretary in 1909: "Under the law these children cannot legally be called neglected … If the Aboriginal child happens to be decently clad and apparently looked after it is very difficult to show that the half-caste or Aboriginal child is actually in a neglected condition, and therefore it is impossible to succeed in court." The Board thought it needed the power to separate children from their parents even where there was no question of neglect.

In 1915 legislation to give the Board precisely this power was debated in the New South Wales parliament. One member of the Assembly, Patrick McGarry, denounced the proposal:

These people are unfortunate because, in the interests of so-called civilisation, we have over-run their country and taken away their domain. We now propose to perpetrate further acts of cruelty upon them by separating the children from their parents. The mothers and fathers of these children love them just as much as the birds and animals of the bush care for their off-spring, and honourable members would not perpetrate a cruelty of this kind even upon an animal.

Notwithstanding McGarry's opposition, supported by two other members, the amending bill was passed with overwhelming support. The Board now had the removal powers it had long wanted, and it went into action. Among New South Wales Aborigines the most hated figure was the determined child remover, the Board member and then inspector, Robert Donaldson.

Margaret Clements was born at Warangesda, near Hay, in 1904. Her parents were both Aborigines of mixed descent, and Margaret grew up on three Aboriginal reserves, Moonahculla, Cumeragunga and Brungle. She was part of a large and close extended family of which her mother was the backbone. Her father, Bill Clements, was an itinerant worker who drifted in and out of his family's life. The family was poor but not desperately so. Although on the reserves and stations, where different Aboriginal clans had come together, the culture of their mother's and father's people was in the process of breaking down, the Clements children, to judge by Margaret's charming memoir written in later years, still lived a distinctively Aboriginal life—listening wide-eyed to the old stories of the spirit world, being treated by traditional remedies, roaming wild, hunting and eating native game. At the same time, the sisters went to school at both Moonahculla and Brungle.

According to the memoir of Margaret Clements, all Aboriginal families feared the police. When police arrived children fled into the bush. At Cumeragunga mothers and their children often swam across the Murray to escape. It was at Brungle that police representing the Protection Board first raised the suggestion that the Clements girls be sent to the training institute at Cootamundra. Their parents absolutely refused. Some time after, when her father had gone off shearing, Margaret's mother took three of her daughters back to Moonahculla.

In 1915, as we have seen, the Aboriginal Protection Board at last received the power it wanted, to separate Aboriginal children from their parents at will. One day in 1917 the police arrived at the school at Moonahculla with orders to pick up the Clements girls. On that day Margaret and May were at school, while the youngest, Genevieve, was in hospital in Deniliquin. Margaret was thirteen at the time, May eleven.

The teacher–manager at Moonahculla, Mr Hill, ordered all other Aboriginal children to leave school. The children must have told their families what was taking place. Some forty or fifty Aborigines soon assembled. Hill's wife was disturbed about the removal of Margaret and May behind their mother's back. She told two boys to go at once to fetch their mother, who was working a mile and a half away. Mrs Hill delayed the girls' departure by insisting they must eat. Margaret's mother ran to the school. Her daughters clung on to her. She insisted, "They are my children and they not go with you." The girls, mistaking a handcuff holster for a gun, thought the policemen might shoot their mother unless they agreed to go.

The policemen allowed Margaret's mother to travel with her daughters in the police car to Deniliquin. Once there, another blow was struck. The police drove straight to the hospital to pick up Genevieve. For the remainder of her life Margaret remembers "the horror on my mother's face and her heart-broken cry". By chance the day before Genevieve had left the hospital with her aunt and uncle. "Mrs Clements, you can have your little girl." Margaret's mother was so grateful for this mercy that, time and again, she kissed the policeman's hand. Margaret and May left their mother at the police station at Deniliquin. Mrs Clements waved frantically as her daughters sped away. What then?

I heard years later how after watching us go out of her life, she wandered away from the police station three miles along the road leading out of the town to Moonahculla. She was worn out, with no food or money, her apron still on. She wandered off the road to rest in the long grass under a tree. That is where old Uncle and Aunt found her next day. They found our mother still moaning and crying. They heard the sounds and thought it was an animal in pain. Uncle stopped the horse and got out of the buggy to investigate. Auntie heard him talking the language. She got down and rushed to old Uncle's side. Mother was half-demented and ill. They gave her water and tried to feed her, but she couldn't eat. She was not interested in anything for weeks, and wouldn't let Genevieve out of her sight. She slowly got better, but I believe for months after, at the sight of a policeman's white helmet coming round the bend of the river, she would find her little girl and escape into the bush, as did all the Aboriginal people who had children.

Margaret and May were trained for domestic service at the Cootamundra Girls' Home. Within two years Margaret was sent out to a "situation" in Sydney. For the first time in her life she felt real fear. Here she was treated with great cruelty, beaten, abused as a worthless black, overworked, kept permanently hungry.

Margaret was able to write to her mother from time to time. She conveyed what she was suffering by drawing pictures. Her mother and father came to Sydney, found out where her daughter worked and visited her. Her father secretly threw his daughter half a crown. Margaret was by now so lonely and starved of affection that the brief reunion with her parents sent her almost crazy with grief. Shortly after her parents had left, she tried to take her life with rat poison. For a few weeks after this incident, her mistress was less cruel. The ill-treatment then resumed.

Eventually Margaret Clements was able to find a new situation in a New South Wales country town. She now met up with her sister May. May had been dealt with even more harshly than Margaret since leaving the Aboriginal training school at Cootamundra. She had with her a revolver.

She told Margaret that she would take her own life if the savage beatings by her present master ever resumed.

Eventually at the age of twenty-one, eight years after being taken from her family, Margaret Clements was permitted by the Protection Board to return to Moonahculla to be with her uncle before he died. Yet to some extent the policy of the Protection Board—to "solve the Aboriginal problem" by "dissociating the children from camp life"—had worked. Margaret soon left for Melbourne to seek employment and later married into a non-Aboriginal family. What the Board could not have predicted, however, was that Margaret Tucker, as she became, would be drawn into Aboriginal politics in Melbourne or that she would write the first important book outlining the terrible cruelty of the child removal policies of Robert Donaldson and the New South Wales Aboriginal Protection Board.

iii. Lorna Cubillo

In 1911, four years before the New South Wales Protection Board won the right to take Aboriginal children from their parents, the Commonwealth government took over from South Australia the administration of the Northern Territory. It began to collect "half-caste" children almost at once. The policy seems to have been the brainchild of an administrator in the Territory, F. E. Goldsmith, and to have been set in place by the first Commonwealth Chief Protector of the Aborigines, Dr Herbert Basedow.

Basedow's scheme for the institutionalisation of the Territory's "half-caste" children received strong support from the Acting Administrator, Samuel James Mitchell. "In my opinion," Mitchell wrote to his Minister in Canberra, "one of the first works to be undertaken is to gather in all the half-caste children who are living with Aborigines. The police could do most of this work. No doubt the mothers would object and there would be an outcry from well-meaning people about depriving the mother of her child but the future of the children should I think outweigh all other considerations." The policy course was struck.

Where, however, were these "half-caste" children to go? In the north of the Territory, the police-protectors who gathered them in brought the children to Darwin, at first to the general Aboriginal reserve, the Kahlin Compound; later, from 1924, in order better to segregate the "half-caste" from the "full blood", they were taken to a nearby three-bedroom house. In what conditions did the Darwin "half-castes" live? In 1927 the superintendent of Kahlin Compound reported thus: "The building is not only too small, but is very much out of repair ... the floor is rotten ... the shower is out of order ... In the kitchen the stove is unfit for use ..." Worst of all was the overcrowding. It is difficult to believe but none the less true that by the late 1920s, seventy-six babies, children and young adults were living in a cottage suitable for a single family. The inmates were locked in for twelve hours or more.

In the southern half of the Territory, in the corrugated iron shed known as the Bungalow, conditions were even worse. In 1924 a journalist visited the Bungalow at Alice Springs. He described the place as "a horror" where the souls of fifty human beings were being destroyed. In 1929 the Reverend Davies visited the Bungalow when it moved to Jay's Creek. "The accommodation provided exhausts my power to paint adequately ... The whole place makes me boil that such a thing can be tolerated in a Christian country."

No-one endowed the sorry business of child removal with a grander social and geo-political purpose than the architect of Aboriginal policy in the Northern Territory between 1927 and 1939, the Chief Protector Dr Cecil Cook. When his protectorship began, no more than 3,000 Europeans were settled in the Territory. They were vastly outnumbered by Aborigines—18,000 "full bloods" and 800 "half-castes". Cook was particularly obsessed by the menace posed to White Australia by the "half-castes". Anxious brooding on rates of birth convinced him that in one or two generations the Territory's "half-castes" would outnumber the whites.

How was such a nightmare to be averted? Dr Cook's plans were clear. All "half-caste" children must continue to be collected by the police and institutionalised in the state-run homes in Darwin and Alice Springs. In these homes the "half-castes" were to be segregated from the "full bloods". The girls were to be given a rudimentary education, trained in the domestic arts and released, at age fourteen or so, into service in respectable white homes. The boys were to be prepared for work as station hands.

Dr Cook, however, was concerned not only with the social but also the biological future of the "half-castes" under his control. As Chief Protector under the Territory ordinance of 1918, Cook wielded immense power over the lives of the Aborigines, including the right to approve or veto marriage. During his protectorship, marriages between "half-castes" and "full bloods" were, in practice, forbidden. More unusually, a vital dimension of Cook's policy was to try to arrange for the marriage of "half-caste" girls to European males. He believed that if the state encouraged marriages between "half-caste" females and white males, over four or five generations the stain of Aboriginal blood could eventually be bred out altogether. Cook was the champion of a policy called "breeding out the colour", or more popularly, "fuck 'em up white".

In 1939 the policy and practice of child removal in the Northern Territory changed gear. Dr Cook had always been a fierce opponent of the Christian missions. His successor, the former colonial administrator of Papua New Guinea W. P. Chinnery, was not. In 1940 Chinnery decided to close the Government's "half-caste" homes in Darwin and Alice Springs and to transfer their inmates to a new Roman Catholic home on Melville Island and a new Methodist home on Croker Island.

As it turned out, these plans were interrupted. After the Japanese bombing of Darwin in January 1942, virtually all the "half-caste" children institutionalised in the Territory were transferred south, chiefly to South Australia (where one group was housed in horse stables at Balaklava) and to New South Wales. At the end of war most of these children returned to the Territory. The Christian island homes reopened. Two new "half-caste" homes were created—the fundamentalist Retta

Dixon Home in Darwin and the Anglican St Mary's Hostel in Alice Springs.

Lorna Napanangka was born in 1938 at Banka Banka Station near Tennant Creek. Her mother was Maudie of the Waramungu people and her father a European soldier named Horace Nelson. Horace abandoned Maudie, who died shortly after Lorna's birth. Lorna was raised by her mother's sister, Maisie, whom she believed to be her biological mother, and by her grandmother. Little is known of Lorna's first years. All that is clear is that Lorna moved at some stage from Banka Banka to a new station depot, Seven Mile Creek; from Seven Mile Creek to Six Mile Creek; and in August 1945, because of lack of water, from there to Phillip Creek.

Phillip Creek was established by the Aborigines Island Mission with the assistance of the Northern Territory Native Affairs Branch. More than 200 Aborigines, of both the Waramungu and Walpiri peoples, settled there. The adults camped around the settlement. When they reached school age the children were separated from their families and placed in dormitories—the "full blood" boys in one; the "full blood" girls in another; the "half-caste" boys and girls in a third. It was in the "half-caste" dormitory that Lorna slept.

There is some uncertainty about whether or not Lorna's "mother", Maisie, lived permanently at Phillip Creek or worked at Banka Banka. There is even some uncertainty about whether or not her grandmother was still alive. What is not uncertain, however, is that Lorna was a happy and healthy child who spoke both the Waramungu and Walpiri tongues but little English and lived among a large, warm extended family at Phillip Creek. There is considerable controversy about how far the "half-caste" children were accepted within the traditional Aboriginal world. There is no controversy, however, with regard to Lorna Napanangka's acceptance by her people. Two "full blood" Aboriginal women who lived at Phillip Creek with Lorna, Bunny and Annie Naparrula, gave evidence in 1999 before a court. They said that all the "half-caste" children at Phillip Creek were fully accepted by their Aboriginal families and dearly loved.

"No-one", Bunny said, "hated these half-caste kids; mothers and step-fathers, they looked after them just like their own."

During the war the policy of collecting the "half-caste" children had, of necessity, been abandoned. After the war the old policy was resumed. By mid-1947 it appeared as if the new "half-caste" home in Darwin, Retta Dixon, had both the room and the staff to take in the sixteen or so "half-caste" children living at Phillip Creek. On 23 July both Amelia Shankelton, the head of Retta Dixon, and Les Penhall, a cadet patrol officer, arrived separately at Phillip Creek. Within a day, the "half-caste" children were loaded onto Penhall's truck and driven away. All the camp was howling for the children, Annie Naparrula remembered. The women in the camp—in the traditional ritual for the mourning of the dead—beat their heads with sticks until they bled. Some women and children locked themselves indoors. Some temporarily left the camp—a place of sorrow. One mother of a child who had been taken was never to return. For the Aborigines who lived at Phillip Creek, the removal of the sixteen "half-caste" children on 14 July 1947 would never be forgotten. One of the children removed was Lorna Napanangka. On the two-day journey to Darwin she nursed an infant, suffering from diarrhoea, less than two years old. Fifty years later Lorna claimed she had never fully recovered her mental balance after the sudden inexplicable loss on that day of her family and her world.

Lorna Nelson, as she was now called, was an inmate of Retta Dixon for the next ten years. Some Aborigines have fond memories of Retta Dixon, especially of Amelia Shankelton and two other female staff. Not Lorna Napanangka. For her Retta Dixon was a place where she was starved of all physical and emotional affection, where her language was beaten out of her, where a regime of joyless, puritanical religiosity prevailed and where the beliefs of people like her mother and grandmother were said to condemn the soul to hell. Lorna's feelings with regard to Amelia Shankelton were ambivalent—a mixture of rebellion and respect. Her feelings with regard to one of the male missionaries—"the chief judge and whipper" as he was once called—were a combination of intense loathing and animal fear. On one occasion this missionary placed his hand high on her thigh. On another occasion, for a trivial breach of the Sabbath rules, he beat Lorna so savagely with a belt and buckle that her face was scarred and her nipple almost torn off. Almost fifty years later this missionary spoke in court with such an air of superior rectitude about how the rod of correction could straighten out a child that it chilled the judge's heart.

During her years at Retta Dixon, Lorna lost almost all contact with her family. Once some relatives approached the Home. Lorna tried to touch their hands across the fence. She was called away and strapped. Shortly before she left Retta Dixon, Lorna Nelson travelled to Banka Banka and Tennant Creek. Although she met Maisie and other family, she found she could no longer even converse freely with them because of her loss of language and divergent life experience. The severance from family was complete.

Lorna Cubillo, as she came to be called after her marriage, settled in Darwin, married a sometimes violent Filipino, bore six children, suffered much ill health and worked as a cleaner and then a clerical assistant until her retirement in 1991.

In 1996 she and Peter Gunner, another "half-caste" Aborigine separated from his family and community as a child, sued the Commonwealth government for wrongful imprisonment and breach of duty of care, among other things. Two psychiatrists who examined her before the trial thought that she had suffered from chronic depression and post-traumatic stress disorder for the remainder of her life as a consequence of her removal. The Gunner–Cubillo case was heard in the Federal Court between 1998 and 2000. In August 2000 Justice O'Loughlin, although far from unsympathetic to her suffering, dismissed her case and that of Peter Gunner on a variety of legal grounds.

iv. Malcolm Charles Smith

In New South Wales in 1940, the power that the Aborigines Protection

Board had acquired in 1915 to remove Aboriginal children at will was withdrawn. The separation of an Aboriginal child from his or her parents was now governed by general child welfare legislation and required the agreement of a court. Even more importantly, over the decades the rationale of the policy and practice of Aboriginal child removal had changed throughout Australia. Before the Second World War, child removal was thought of as an exercise in racial–social engineering, a way of finding a solution to the "problem" of the Aborigines. After the war it changed gradually into an administrative habit, the more or less routine response of police, welfare workers and the courts to the difficulties Aboriginal families so frequently faced. In this era Aboriginal child removal was an instrument of assimilation. It was also the expression of something no less destructive but altogether more banal—a racism rooted in the shallow soil of indifference and thoughtlessness.

Malcolm Smith grew up along the Darling River, one of thirteen children born to Joe and Gladys, respectively of Ngyiampaa and Pankantji descent. In order to maintain their freedom and to avoid the tedium of life on one of the New South Wales stations or reserves, Joe and Gladys kept on the move throughout their early married life, taking all they possessed in a horse-drawn cart, sleeping under a tarpaulin. Eventually they and their children settled in a shack they built at the Old Dareton Mission, as it was called, a rough Aboriginal camp without a water supply or electricity but also without the presence of a European manager to interfere in their lives.

Throughout these years Joe worked as a musterer, saw-miller, fruit-picker and rabbiter; Gladys, who had lost a hand in a shooting accident at the age of sixteen, tended the children with love and care. The most conspicuous success of the couple was their ability to avoid, throughout their years together, the attention of welfare and the police. This was a time, as Joe would later put it, when "we used to dodge welfare people because all Aboriginal people knew they used to take the children away."

In 1965 Gladys died. Malcolm was eleven years old at the time, a carefree boy who swam in the irrigation channels, hunted birds with his shanghai and who, while enrolled, very rarely went to school. Although they helped their father out at times with the young ones, the older girls of the Smith family were beginning to have babies of their own. When he went fruit picking, Joe would take his six youngest children, all boys, along with him.

On one occasion Malcolm and his elder brother Robert stole bicycles from the local high school. Joe returned the bikes and gave his sons a belting. Nonetheless the police arrested Malcolm and Robert. They were charged at Wentworth with being in a condition of neglect. Joe attended the hearing, but without legal representation. He barely understood what was taking place. His sons were found guilty and sent to Kinchela Aboriginal Boys' Home near Kempsey, 1,500 kilometres away. Joe had no idea where his boys had been sent. He was illiterate and had never written a letter in his life. Moreover, after the death of Gladys he turned to drink. Soon after, he also lost control of his four youngest sons to a Salvation Army home in Melbourne, although they, unlike Robert and Malcolm, never lost contact with their family at Dareton, going home each Christmas for holidays. Unlike their two older brothers, none of them ever fell into serious trouble with the law.

Malcolm from the age of eleven lived in institutions. He endured first the dreary routine of Kinchela and then, after his release and his immediate involvement in petty crime, the punitive regime of Mt Penang and the brutal regime of Tamworth Boys' Home, the toughest youth prison in the State. In 1972, for the first time since his incarceration, the authorities decided to contact Malcolm Smith's family. His father was keen to have him back. The prison authorities noticed that his spirits lifted at once. In early 1973 Malcolm returned to Dareton. It was his first contact with any member of his family, except for Robert, in seven years. He and his family had a lot of catching up to do.

At Dareton, Malcolm Smith returned almost at once to his life of petty, impulsive property crime. In the years between 1973 and 1980 his life became a series of substantial prison terms punctuated by the briefest periods of freedom. In 1980, while inside, Malcolm began receiving letters from home which told of how one of his sisters, Peggy, was being bashed and harassed by her white boyfriend, Terry Percival. Malcolm took it into his head that as soon as he was free he would act as the protector of his sister as he had been the protector of several fellow-prisoners over the years. On release Malcolm Smith found Terry Percival in a pub, took him outside and beat him to death on the footpath. It was the first really violent or serious crime he had committed in his life. When he was arrested he discovered, to his dismay, that members of his family were appalled by what he had done. They disowned him altogether. When he went to trial for the killing of Percival, several gave evidence against him, including Peggy and his father, Joe. Malcolm was found guilty of manslaughter, and returned to gaol.

Malcolm Smith's life now changed. In various prisons in New South Wales he suffered a series of psychotic breakdowns. One psychiatrist who later examined his case, Dr Rodney Milton, thought he was most likely crushed by his family's rejection of him and overwhelmed by feelings of remorse and guilt. Malcolm now took to Christianity, listening incessantly to Bible tapes in his cell and carrying a Bible on his person although he could not read. At some moments, when delusional, he believed that he was Jesus Christ and that he was being crucified. At some moments he was very violent. At yet other moments, more common, he began to inflict upon himself serious physical harm. Malcolm became increasingly obsessed by a passage from the Gospel of St Matthew, chapter 5, verse 29: "If thy eye offends thee, pluck it out." In September 1982 he gouged out his left eye with such force that he lost the sight of it permanently. When he was less tormented Malcolm painted pictures, either with an Aboriginal or a Christian theme.

On 29 December 1982 Malcolm Smith took a paintbrush into a toilet cubicle. Hal Wootten, one of the Royal Commissioners into Aboriginal Deaths in Custody, who later examined his case and on whose wise and humane report I have relied for my interpretation of his life, recorded what happened to Malcolm Smith: "[The warders] found Malcolm kneeling on the floor near the toilet pan, muttering something that sounded like 'Oh God.' They saw the bristles and metal sleeve of a paint brush protruding from his eye." A week later he was pronounced dead.

God only knows what would have happened to Malcolm Smith if he had been with his family during his teenage years. All we know is that at the age of eleven he was a healthy and a happy boy and that, as a consequence of stealing a bike, he was removed from all contact with his family for the next seven years. In the post-war years, the separation of Aboriginal children from their families by the authorities had become little more than a reflex action when difficulties arose. For this habit of the authorities, Malcolm Smith, and many thousands of other children, would pay a truly terrible price.

HOW MANY?

What proportion of Aboriginal children born before 1970 were removed from their parents and families in the years when the policy of separation was most intensely applied? Although Bringing them home did not attempt to name a precise figure, it did argue that somewhere between one in three and one in ten Aboriginal children had been separated from their families between 1910 and 1970. The "one in three" possibility was derived from a number of local studies. In the late 1980s Dr Jane McKendrick surveyed the patients who visited the Aboriginal Health Service in Melbourne. She found that one-third had been removed from their parents as children. At the same time Dr Eric Hunter conducted a survey of adult Aborigines in the Kimberleys in Western Australia. One quarter of the elderly and one in seven of the middle-aged told him they had been separated from their families as children. A decade or so earlier Dr Max Kamien surveyed 320 adults in the town of Bourke in New South Wales. The authors of Bringing them home mistakenly believed he found that one in three had been separated from both their parents as children. In fact he found that one in three had been separated from one parent, while 5% of males and 7% of females had been separated from both. Of all the small studies relied on by *Bringing them home* only McKendrick's is consistent with a finding of one in three removals. It is, of course, impossible to generalise across the States and across the decades from so narrow a base. The one in three upper limit for child removal suggested by *Bringing them home* is certainly wrong.

The lower estimate of one in ten is far more soundly based. In 1994 the Australian Bureau of Statistics conducted a rigorously scientific survey of the self-identified indigenous population of Australia. It found that 1.6% of those of fourteen years or under, 4.6% of those between fifteen and twenty-five; 10.1% of those between twenty-five and forty-four; and 10.6% of those older than forty-four had been separated as children from their natural families by missions or governments or welfare. It seems clear from this survey that about 10% of all Aboriginal children born before 1970 were removed from their families; that the proportion of separated Aboriginal children born in the decade after 1970 more than halved; and that among those born after 1980 the proportion of Aboriginal children separated from their family, although still several times higher than for the population as a whole, was only one-sixth of what it had been during the critical Aboriginal child separation decades before 1970. No-one can be sure whether the percentage of Aboriginal children removed in the period before 1930 was as high as the percentage separated between 1930 and 1950. Nor can anyone be sure how many Aboriginal children had been so successfully absorbed or assimilated into the European population that they no longer identified themselves as indigenous at the time the ABS survey was conducted in 1994. Nonetheless it still seems as safe as any rough estimate can be that no fewer than one in ten of all Aboriginal children were separated, for whatever reason, from their families between 1910 and 1970.

In absolute numbers, then, how many Aboriginal children were separated during these years? Concerning this question considerable confusion exists. One figure produced frequently in the very early stages of the stolen generations debate was 100,000. This figure was based on a misunderstanding of a claim once made by Peter Read, namely that child removal may have been responsible for as many as 100,000 Australians now alive not identifying themselves with their Aboriginality. Right-wing commentators have made merry with the figure of 100,000, even suggesting, on what basis I do not know, that it was deliberately chosen as a means of linking the stolen generations with the Holocaust—100,000 separated children standing, so it is claimed, in the same proportion to the Aboriginal population as the six million murdered Jews did in relation to the overall population of world Jewry during the period of Nazi rule.

Because of the misunderstanding arising from his figure of 100,000, and the ideological mischief made of it, in his book *rape of the soul so profound* Peter Read made a new estimate of 50,000 to put in its place. This is almost certainly also an exaggeration. Read examined the files concerning New South Wales Aboriginal child removal between 1883 and 1969 and arrived at a removal figure of 5,625. Thinking this to be an underestimate, he guessed, on the assumption that 15% of removals in New South Wales were of Aborigines, that 10,000 would be closer to the mark. By extrapolating from New South Wales to the country as a whole, he then arrived at a figure of 50,000. However, even if the 10,000 figure is right, the extrapolation to 50,000 seems too large. In two of the major areas of Aboriginal population—Queensland and the Northern Territory—the proportion of Aboriginal children removed was far smaller than the proportion in New South Wales. In Queensland it was common to remove whole families or even communities to missions or reserves but relatively rare after about 1915 to separate children from mothers or parents, except in the dormitory system on the mission stations or government reserves. Queensland was the only State with a large Aboriginal population and no special purpose "half-caste" children's home. In the Northern Territory, although "half-caste" children were systematically removed, "half-castes" were a small proportion of the Aboriginal population as a whole. Between 1910 and 1970 it is likely that fewer than 1,000 removals were effected in the Territory. I do not know of any estimates of child removals in Western Australia, the other State with a sizeable Aboriginal population in which very many separations occurred. Nevertheless it seems to me impossible that what took place there could make the figure of 50,000 removals even remotely right.

As we have seen, the Australian Bureau of Statistics assessed the number of Aborigines alive in 1994 who said they had been separated from their families as children. In numbers they found about 17,000 removals. Of these about 4,500 occurred after 1970. It is not easy to estimate how many Aborigines born after 1900 had died by 1994. Extrapolating from this figure on the basis of Aboriginal life expectancy makes it seem probable that between 20,000 and 25,000 Aboriginal children were separated from their families between 1910 and 1970. In its submission to the Senate in May 2000, the Howard government implied that the Australian public had been misled over the stolen generations issue because "only" one in ten Aboriginal children had been separated from their families over a period of seventy years. Only! Given the stunning cruelty and injustice so often involved, and the ripple effect of the removals on parents, siblings and extended families, 20,000 or 25,000 separations seems to me a far from trifling sum.

Virtually no reliable generalisation about the nature of these removals can be made. Many of the children separated from their mothers, especially in the early decades of the policy in Queensland, the Northern Territory and the desert regions of South Australia, were first generation, so-called "half-castes", born of tribal mothers and European (or occasionally Chinese) fathers. Many others were children of mixed descent, who lived on Aboriginal settlements or on the outskirts of the country towns, especially in New South Wales, Victoria and the southern areas of South and Western Australia.

Some Aboriginal children, especially in the inter-war period, were removed under State or Commonwealth laws that made the Chief Protectors of Aborigines or the Aboriginal Protection Boards the legal guardians of all Aboriginal children in their jurisdiction. Some, especially after the Second World War, were separated from their families by the operation of the general child welfare legislation in their States. Some separated Aboriginal children were sent to special purpose institutions established in their States. Some were sent to Aboriginal missions established by the churches. Some were placed in dormitories on general Aboriginal reserves. Some were sent to general institutions for orphans or neglected children. Some were sent to foster homes. Some were formally adopted.

Some separated children lost all contact with their families, cultures and communities, either through state intent or state indifference. Some maintained regular contact with families, say at Christmas time. Some were separated, in the later years of the policy, because they were assessed by welfare authorities as being at risk. Some were removed from families—chaotic and impoverished from the European point of view—in which they experienced great love and attentive care. Some children were removed from their families when they were very young; some in the late teenage years. Some were trained as domestic servants or menial labourers. Some were given a primary education of a more conventional kind.

Concerning the separated Aboriginal children—over the decades and between the States—only one generalisation holds good. Virtually none of the separated children were tribal "full bloods". Virtually all were those who were once called "half-castes" and are now called Aborigines of mixed descent.

SOME QUESTIONS ABOUT BRINGING THEM HOME

Bringing them home had a profound effect on public opinion. It was not, however, a flawless report. This was hardly surprising. The policy and practice of Aboriginal child removal had not even been identified as a discrete historical problem until Peter Read published his seminal essay "The Stolen Generations" in 1981. More importantly still, at the time the Human Rights and Equal Opportunity Commission conducted its inquiry no reliable history of child removal existed. As a consequence the authors of Bringing them home were obliged to cobble together their general history and particular histories of what occurred in the Northern Territory and the States from a wide variety of narrow studies and from the reports of the historians and public servants commissioned by the State governments to assist them in their task. The historical chapters in Bringing them home were of uneven quality. In them there was, too, a gulf between the seriousness of the moral issues involved and the thinness of the historical grasp. No-one could read these chapters without recognising the need for further research and thought.

It was also clear and understandable that the authors of Bringing them home had been shaken by the experience of listening to the hundreds of Aboriginal witnesses who appeared before the inquiry and who told their stories—often for the first time, often at great personal cost, often with tears in their eyes—of desolating fear and abandonment, of institutional coldness and brutality, of physical, moral and sexual abuse. One of the great virtues of Bringing them home was that it gave the victims of child removal a public voice and allowed non-indigenous Australians to listen to stories of cruelties they had never before understood. Nonetheless the anger and shame the authors of Bringing them home experienced during the course of their inquiry was not without its cost.

In claiming that as many as one in three Aboriginal children might have been removed from their families between 1910 and 1970, Bringing them home greatly exaggerated the numbers of children involved. Because many Aborigines are today, for good reason, deeply offended by the racial distinction between Aborigines of full or mixed descent, Bringing them home tended to treat this issue too delicately, leaving the removal policy unnecessarily obscure. At times readers would have understood that removal policies affected only Aborigines of mixed descent. At other times they might have believed that the policy of separation involved all Aboriginal children, irrespective of whether or not they were, in the ugly racist language of the day, "full bloods" or "half-castes". Bringing them home also failed to distinguish with sufficient clarity between the pre-war eugenicist and the post-war assimilationist chapters of child removal. As a consequence it failed to distinguish between the time when "half-caste" children were removed in order to help "breed out" the colour or to take them away from the "degraded" life of the "blacks' camps", and the time when racist and welfarist motives for the removal of children were, in complicated ways, intertwined. This was no minor matter. Through the failure to distinguish clearly between removals in the age of eugenics, biological absorption and racial engineering, and removals in the age of social and cultural assimilation, the plausibility of the discussion of the relationship between child removal and genocide in Bringing them home was, as I shall argue, weakened.

Some other problems arose. The inquiry could have benefited—and made itself less vulnerable to subsequent attack—if it had been more active in soliciting the evidence of the public servants, policemen, patrol officers and missionaries who were involved in the policy of child removal. It could also have defused much subsequent criticism if it had more explicitly acknowledged in its report something anyhow obvious to commonsense, namely that while the testimony of the Aborigines who were removed as children was by far the most important source of understanding, and that the evidence of what the children experienced and suffered would be found in no government or church file, nonetheless the memories of some members of the stolen generations, like all childhood memories, were likely to have been simplified and even distorted with the passage of time.

Bringing them home is best seen, then, as the first move in an attempt at understanding. It is definitely not the final word. After its publication two possibilities existed. One was that an extended national discussion would be conducted in which understanding would be tested and refined. The other was that the issue of the stolen generations and the assessment of *Bringing them home* would be overtaken by a bitter, polemical struggle between left and right. It was this second possibility which came to pass. Soon after its publication, from within the small right-wing intelligentsia in Australia, the campaign against *Bringing them home* began.

BETRAYING THE VICTIMS — RON BRUNTON

The first serious blow in this campaign was struck by Ron Brunton, resident anthropologist at the private enterprise think-tank, the Institute of Public Affairs. Brunton has come to dominate a certain niche market in the nation's ideological affairs. Whenever a significant judgment or report conspicuously sympathetic to the Aborigines is published, it is not long before he puts together a response. Previously Brunton had written scathing criticisms of Mabo and the Royal Commission into Aboriginal Deaths in Custody. Six months or so after *Bringing them home* was published, Brunton's reply, *Betraying the Victims*, appeared.

In *Betraying the Victims* Brunton accepted that very many Aboriginal children had been separated from their mothers and communities by force. He gently chided some fellow members of the right for their inability to see how such forcible child removal offended against a value that all conservatives ought to hold dear—the defence of the family against the interventionist nanny state. Nonetheless the central thrust of his pamphlet was the suggestion that in its failure to mount a precise, careful and sober case the authors of *Bringing them home* had betrayed the victims of child removal policies "almost as surely" as if they had written a report denying that forced removal had occurred. Sir Ronald Wilson and Mick Dodson had let the Aborigines down. Ron Brunton was apparently their true friend.

I do not wish to deny that at least some of Brunton's criticisms deserve a considered response. Brunton argues in *Betraying the Victims* that the tendency of *Bringing them home* is to discount the possibility that at least some of the children who were taken from their families were removed because the welfare authorities had genuine grounds for believing the children were at risk. He also argues that *Bringing them home* tends too readily to discount in advance the possibility that some children were relinquished voluntarily by their parents and not as a result of force or pressure or undue influence. On both these issues Brunton's arguments are crude. He does not understand the complexity of the relationship between racist and welfarist thinking in an era where the ambition of policy was to assimilate a people assumed to be inferior. Nor does he understand that the maintenance of what he calls "moral agency" for a people dispossessed of their land and culture, discriminated against in law, and treated with systematic racial condescension, is no simple thing. Nevertheless on both these issues—of justification for removal and voluntary relinquishment—Brunton has a point. *Bringing them home* burns with a fierce sympathy for the suffering of the separated Aborigine children. If Brunton had done nothing more than point to the dangers of oversimplification to which, as a consequence of its passion, *Bringing them home* was prone, his pamphlet could have played a useful corrective role.

Unfortunately Brunton did not limit himself in this way. Most of his methodological criticisms are of a nit-picking or point-scoring kind. Brunton accuses the authors of *Bringing them home* of seriously and perhaps deliberately distorting the outcome of their inquiry because of the fact that of the 535 Aboriginal witnesses they heard, "only 143" were quoted directly in their report. Only? *Bringing them home* is almost 700 pages long. One of the reasons it is so interesting is the amount of space it devotes to lengthy extracts from the evidence that it heard. If *Bringing them home* had quoted from all its witnesses it would have been interminable. Undoubtedly many of the Aboriginal witnesses who were questioned told stories of a similar kind. To claim, as Brunton does, that the witnesses who were not quoted directly were "largely ignored" is baseless. How could he know? Moreover to hint, as Brunton does, at the "disturbing possibility" that Aboriginal witnesses whose experiences at separation were positive were deliberately excluded from the final report is nothing more than a slur on the authors of *Bringing them home*. Brunton might care to examine the *Forde Commission of Inquiry into Abuse of Children in Queensland Institutions*, published in 1999. If he did so he would find that it quotes directly from far fewer of its witnesses to abuse than *Bringing them home* does, that it is far less precise than *Bringing them home* is in identifying these witnesses, and that its account of the conditions in the Queensland institutions is even more uniformly negative than the parallel accounts given in *Bringing them home*. So far as I am aware, no-one, and certainly not Ron Brunton who lives in Queensland, has accused the Forde inquiry of "largely ignoring" the many witnesses it does not directly cite. So far as I am aware no-one has raised "the disturbing possibility" that the Forde inquiry might have deliberately suppressed positive accounts given to it about conditions in Queensland's child institutions. And so far as I am aware no-one has spoken, with regard to the witnesses to the Forde inquiry, about "the role of suggestion in creating false memories of events that never actually happened", as Brunton thought fit to do with regard to the Aborigines who spoke of their experiences to the Wilson–Dodson inquiry.

Some of Brunton's other methodological criticism is not so much mean-spirited as impractical. Brunton criticises the Wilson–Dodson inquiry for failing to test the evidence of the Aboriginal witnesses who appeared before it against the documentary evidence on their cases held in government files. He contrasts this with the work of the Royal Commission into Aboriginal Deaths in Custody (of which, incidentally, he was once highly critical too). In this comparison he fails to consider two crucial facts. The authors of *Bringing them home* heard from 535 Aboriginal witnesses; the Deaths in Custody Royal Commission was charged with investigating the fate of ninety-nine. For its work the Wilson–Dodson inquiry was provided with less than $2 million; Deaths in Custody cost $30 million or more. Archival research into individual case histories is time-consuming, expensive and often fruitless. In defending itself in the case of Lorna Cubillo, the Commonwealth spent a small fortune digging for evidence about the removals at Phillip Creek and ended up failing to locate even one relevant file. Archival investigation of the kind Brunton recommends would have been, for the Wilson–Dodson inquiry, an impossibly expensive exercise.

Even if, however, they had been able to afford this kind of investigation, and had discovered relevant material as a result, the consequences would not have been as straightforwardly beneficial as Brunton assumes. The greatest contribution of the Wilson–Dodson inquiry was the creation of an atmosphere in which the victims of the removal policies felt confident in telling their stories. As a consequence the nation was able to hear, for the first time, the voices of the victims and their stories of abuse, bewilderment, disorientation, loneliness and pain. If the inquiry had been conducted in the manner of a Royal Commission or a court of law—where discrepancies between the stories of witnesses and the government records concerning them are tested under cross-examination by lawyers—the goodwill on which the inquiry relied would have evaporated very quickly indeed. No doubt there were costs in the decision of Sir Ronald Wilson and Mick Dodson to listen to the witnesses rather than to interrogate them. What Brunton does not understand, however, is that there were very great benefits as well.

Some of Brunton's methodological criticism of Bringing them home is plainly ridiculous. Consider the following example. Brunton is aware that the Wilson–Dodson inquiry was established to investigate Aboriginal child removal, a phenomenon involving perhaps 25,000 cases, occurring in every Australian State and territory over a period of sixty or seventy years. He must also be aware that it had available $2 million in funding. Nevertheless he argues that it was remiss of it, and even a little sinister, that it did not go back to the Keating government to ask for amended terms of reference so that it could investigate, in addition to Aboriginal child removal, all cases of non-Aboriginal child removals as well, including even the case of the removal of British children to Australia both before and after the Second World War. This is self-evidently absurd. So, too, is the implication behind Brunton's criticism, namely that a comparison between Aboriginal and non-Aboriginal child removal involves a comparison of "like with like". We know that about 10% of Aboriginal children were separated from their families between 1910 and 1970. I would be very surprised if the number of non-Aboriginal child removals in the equivalent period came to even 1%. We know that as late as the 1950s substantial numbers of Aboriginal children could be removed at the discretion of Chief Protectors or Protection Boards without the permission of parents or reference to a court. Does Brunton really think a full-scale inquiry into non-Aboriginal child removal practices was required to show that such policy applied to Aborigines alone?

It is the question of *Bringing them home* and genocide that here preoccupies Brunton. He argues that if the Wilson–Dodson inquiry had investigated non-Aboriginal child removals its findings about "genocide" would have been even more difficult to sustain. It is to his unsatisfactory treatment of this complicated issue that we must now turn.

The authors of *Bringing them home* argued that in their child removal policies the Commonwealth and State governments, probably after 1946, and certainly after 1951, were according to international law guilty of the crime of genocide, that is to say of the intention to destroy a people, in whole or in part. According to the UN Convention on the Prevention and Punishment of the Crime of Genocide, one means by which this crime can be committed is by the removal of the children of the targeted group. *Bringing them home* argued that the most fundamental purpose of Aboriginal child removal in Australia was their "absorption or assimilation" into European society in order "to acculturate and to socialise" the children "into Anglo-Australian values and aspirations". On the foundation of a variety of legal authorities it argued that the crime of genocide can be committed even where the intention to destroy the group fails; where the destructive intent focuses only on a part of the targeted group; and where the motives of those carrying out the plans are "mixed", for example when plans to destroy the group are not driven solely by "animosity or hatred".

The authors of *Bringing them home* cited the words of a Venezuelan delegate to the United Nations:

> The forced transfer of children to a group where they would be given an education different from that of their own group, and would have new customs, a new religion and probably a new language, was in practice tantamount to the destruction of their group, whose future depended on that generation of children. Such transfer might be made from a group with a low standard of civilisation ... to a highly civilised group ... yet if the intent of the transfer were the destruction of the group, a crime of genocide would undoubtedly have been committed.

As readers of Brunton's pamphlet have by now every reason to expect, several of his criticisms of *Bringing them home* on the question of genocide involve little more than point scoring. Let one example suffice.

In preparation for his attack on *Bringing them home*, Brunton discovered in a manifesto published in 1938 by two Aboriginal activists, Jack Patten and William Ferguson, a passage which argued that in two or three generations the mating of "half-castes" with Europeans without even the danger of "throwback" offered the most rational solution to the problem of the Aborigines. The authors of *Bringing them home* had quoted other passages from this manifesto, about the extermination of the blacks. Given that the policy of "breeding out the colour" was so important an element in their argument about genocide why did they not, Brunton asks, quote this awkward passage as well? Brunton appears to have been extremely pleased with this discovery. There has scarcely been an occasion in his discussion of *Bringing them home* when he has not returned to it.

Like Brunton I find this passage interesting. Is it not strange that two powerful Aboriginal political activists had apparently so internalised the world view of white Australians that it had come to seem to them almost natural to think of the dilution of their Aboriginal blood as the best solution to the problem for Australia their continued existence posed? Or perhaps there is another explanation of this passage. The manifesto written by Jack Patten and William Ferguson was the idea of the pro-Nazi literary critic, P. R. "Inky" Stephensen. According to his biographer, Craig Munro, Stephensen was in the habit of "helping" his Aboriginal political friends to "write and produce ... posters, manifestos and press releases". According to him, moreover, the Patten–Ferguson manifesto bore "the unmistakable signs of Stephensen's aggressive style". Stephensen's magazine, *The Publicist*, was a champion of the eugenic idea of the biological absorption of the Aborigines. Was it not possible that he had insinuated into the manifesto some ideas of his own?

Unlike Brunton I do not think the non-appearance of this passage undermines the credibility of *Bringing them home*. There are many reasons why the authors might not have believed it worth quoting. Even more importantly, unlike Brunton I do not think it helps resolve, one way or the other, the question of the relationship between Aboriginal child removal and genocide. In order to investigate this question it is necessary to leave for a moment both *Bringing them home*'s genocide argument and Ron Brunton's critique.

Concerning genocide no-one has taken us more quickly to the heart of the matter than Hannah Arendt in *Eichmann in Jerusalem*. Arendt argues here that genocide occurred when one people decided it had the right to eliminate another people, in its entirety, and when it began to take action on that belief. It followed from what Arendt wrote that those who advocated the elimination of a distinct people were implicated in genocidal thinking and that those who acted upon such a belief were guilty of genocidal crime. Arendt's is not the only concept of genocide. It is however the one which throws the most valuable light on the discussion of genocide and the stolen generations.

One of the most common misunderstandings concerning genocide is that killing is the only means by which the crime can be committed. This is not only legally but also conceptually wrong. In the course of the debate about genocide and the stolen generations, Raimond Gaita asked whether, if all the members of a nation or an ethnic group were sterilised by the state, this would or would not constitute a crime of genocide. To his question he received, from Brunton and the right-wing intelligentsia, no reply. Nor is genocide, as Brunton seems to believe, merely a new term to describe political killings on a massive scale. Although Pol Pot murdered millions of Cambodians, he was not guilty of genocide, at least in the Arendtian sense, because there is no evidence that he was attempting to wipe a distinct people from the face of the earth.

In both the work of the authors of *Bringing them home* and the response of Ron Brunton, we find considerable confusion with regard to the question of genocide and the stolen generations. The basis of this confusion is the failure to distinguish between the motives of the policy makers before and after the Second World War.

Before the Second World War, the removal of "half-caste" children from Aboriginal camps and settlements was frequently driven by a determination to "solve" the "problem" of the Aborigines once and for all. At this time those in charge of Aboriginal policy generally believed that the tribal "full blood" could not survive contact with a more advanced civilisation. Each year the number of "full bloods" declined. Eventually they were doomed. What the same people noticed, however, was that the numbers of "half-castes" were beginning, in some States, to rise rather rapidly. In their decline the "full bloods" excited both the curiosity of the anthropologists—who wanted to study them before it was too late—and, to some extent, the pity of the general public. In their rise the "half-castes" excited mainly distaste and fear. Some of the most repellent expressions of racism in Australia's history occurred in connection with them. The former Northern Territory constable M.C. Willshire wrote in 1896: "The mongrel half-caste inherits only the vices of civilisation ... If it is a male he is born for the gallows or to be shot; if a female she becomes a wanton devoid of shame. I hold out no gleam of hope for such a repulsive breed." It was commonly argued that "half-castes" had inherited the worst human qualities of both Aborigine and European. It was frequently asserted that their presence undermined social cohesion and the White Australia dream. For those with an interest in Aboriginal administration, "the solution of the half-caste problem" was the first and most troubling item on the agenda of current debate.

It is here that thinking of a genocidal kind emerges. Occasionally public officials advocated the sterilisation of all the half-castes in a State, as did Lothar Gall, the under-secretary at the Home Department in Queensland. Far more commonly, however, the responsible officials—like the Chief Protectors in Western Australia and the Northern Territory, A. O. Neville and Cecil Cook—advocated a complex program of eugenics involving, among other things, the effective prohibition of mating between "full bloods" and "half-castes"; the systematic removal of the "half-caste" children from their families and the "degraded" life of the blacks' camp; the encouragement of marriage between "half-caste" females and white males. Such administrators called this the program of "breeding out the colour".

The leading administrators of Aboriginal affairs assembled in Canberra in April 1937. Their first and most important resolution advocated the "absorption" of the "half-caste"—but not of the "full blood", they stressed—into the European world. The dominant personality at the 1937 conference was A. O. Neville. He explained to a journalist the conference's most important conclusion:

> Mr Neville holds the view that within one hundred years the pure black will be extinct. But the half-caste problem was increasing every year. Therefore their idea was to keep the pure blacks segregated and absorb the half-castes into the white population … The pure black was not a quick breeder. On the other hand the half-caste was. In Western Australia there were half-caste families of twenty and upwards. That showed the magnitude of the problem.
> In order to secure the complete segregation of the children … [they] were left with their mothers [only] until they were two years old. After that they were taken from their mothers and reared in accordance with white ideas.

It was a combination of the beliefs—in the inevitability of the extinction of the "full blood" Aborigine and the desirability of the biological absorption of the "half-caste"—that allowed A. O. Neville to ask the 1937 conference of Aboriginal administrators, "Are we going to have a population of one million blacks in the Commonwealth or are we going to merge them into our white community and eventually forget that there were any Aborigines in Australia?" At this moment in Australian history genocidal thought and administrative practice touched.

After the Second World War the practice of Aboriginal child removal continued. In certain very fundamental ways, however, the thinking of the policy makers had changed. Perhaps because of its association with Nazism, racial eugenics was utterly discredited. Virtually no-one talked any longer about a policy of "breeding out the colour". The policy of the biological absorption of the "half-caste" was replaced by the policy of the cultural assimilation of the Aboriginal people as a whole. Without child removal the policy of biological absorption was unimaginable. Even without child removal the policy of assimilation could have been pursued. Before the war Aboriginal child removal was seen as part of the solution of the problem of the "half-caste". After the war it was commonly seen as a response of welfare authorities to the predictable problems into which so many Aboriginal families fell. Although in the age of assimilation child removal was still racist and paternalistic, in its ingrained assumption that the children were best off if they could be merged into the European world, and although Aboriginal families suffered no less severely when their children were taken from them, the genocidal dimension in the thinking of the inter-war generation of Aboriginal administrators had passed.

It is the failure to distinguish between the policies of "absorption" and "assimilation" and between the philosophies of A. O. Neville and Paul Hasluck, that leads the authors of Bringing them home into the misleading claim that the post-war child removal policies were driven by genocidal intentions. Similarly it is the failure to distinguish between the policy of biological absorption and the policy of socio-cultural assimilation that leads Ron Brunton to the false counter-claim that all talk about genocide and the stolen generations is fatuous and un-Australian. In the thousands of words he has written on the question of genocide and the stolen generations Brunton has never shown a capacity to understand, let alone answer, the arguments developed since 1997 by Raimond Gaita and by me.

For a people that has not yet come to terms with the extremity of what it has done to the indigenous population of Australia, discussion of genocide and the stolen generations was never going to be easy. It was, in fact, made even more difficult by the sneering and contemptuous tone Brunton and his allies adopted during the course of the stolen generations debate. Shortly after he published *Betraying the Victims* Brunton wrote a summary for *Quadrant* magazine. In it he described, humourlessly and at tedious length, an imagined future inquiry into the "unconceived generations", charging those advising Aborigines on methods of birth control with the crime of genocide. Brunton apparently could see no difference between prescribing the pill and forcibly removing children with the purpose of making a people disappear. Moreover each time Brunton wrote about this issue, his language became more extreme. In his original pamphlet he claimed merely that *Bringing them home* was "one of the most intellectually and morally irresponsible documents produced in recent years". In his first *Quadrant* article he called upon the political parties in Australia "to condemn the authors of *Bringing them home*" and to require them to apologise "for their calumnies". The political parties did not respond. As an alternative, in his second *Quadrant* article published late in 2000, Brunton appealed to the Howard government to rid the nation altogether of the obnoxious Human Rights and Equal Opportunities Commission.

Even before *Bringing them home* was published the Howard government encouraged a whispering campaign against the character of Sir Ronald Wilson and his supposed conflict of interest in conducting this inquiry. Brunton responded with enthusiasm. According to Brunton, as Wilson had once been a Presbyterian elder and had been on the board of the

Perth "quarter caste" home, Sister Kate's, he was in danger either of being seen to be protecting the financial interests of his church or of relieving his conscience of guilt. Apparently Brunton could not see that coming from an anthropologist with a track record like his on Aboriginal affairs—Brunton had worked as a consultant for mining companies fighting native title claims and was retained by a private enterprise think-tank supported by mining money—his allegations of conflict of interest with regard to Ronald Wilson might seem to others a touch bizarre.

As we have seen, the opening gambit of Brunton's pamphlet was the claim that *Bringing them home* had exposed the victims of forcible child removal to the malice of those who would exploit the report's weaknesses to deny their suffering. This opening gambit was disingenuous in two distinct ways. At the time he published his pamphlet, public opinion overwhelmingly accepted the truthfulness and moral seriousness of what *Bringing them home* revealed. Brunton was, then, critical of *Bringing them home* for exposing the Aboriginal victims of child removal to precisely the kind of mean-spirited and nit-picking criticism he had pioneered. Yet Brunton's disingenuousness went deeper still. Not long after his pamphlet was published, voices were heard arguing either that the stolen generations issue was a hoax or that, as the separated Aboriginal children had not been stolen but "rescued", they ought to be grateful for what had occurred. These were precisely the kind of people Brunton had warned about. Not only did he not oppose them. Soon he was found speaking on the same platforms and joining with them in an orchestrated campaign.

OLD MEN FORGET

In the early 1980s, well before the time Aboriginal child removal became a public issue, some of the old-timers who had worked in the Native Affairs Branch in Darwin were interviewed for the Oral History Unit of the Northern Territory's Archives Service. Almost all expressed shame and regret at the policy they had been required to implement.

Gordon Sweeney was one of the Territory's most respected patrol officers during and after the Second World War. He described the inter-war child removal policy administered by Dr Cook as a "rather cruel sort of business". All the "half-caste" girls, he said, were brought to Darwin by police officers. They "simply came to a cattle station" and "picked the child up". The mothers could do nothing; they "just had to put up with it". According to Sweeney this cruel policy continued into the post-war period. Eventually a more humane removal policy was introduced. Mothers, and occasionally fathers, were allowed to accompany their children to the compound at Darwin and stay with them until convinced that the child would be all right.

Ted Evans was another highly respected patrol officer. Before 1949 he had, he said, been involved in "the removal of half-caste kiddies". Even now, thirty years later, Aborigines would approach him to ask after the children he had removed. Evans said he had made a real effort to keep in touch with the children he had separated from families and communities. He was thankful that they did not bear him any grudge. In retrospect all of this "saddened" him deeply. Evans claimed that, in the end, he had simply "refused to obey instructions". He was referring here to a report he wrote in 1949 after a group of Aboriginal children was taken from Wave Hill by plane. Its first sentence read: "The removal of the children ... was accompanied by distressing scenes the like of which I wish never to experience again." According to Evans the removal policy was "traumatic, really traumatic for all sides, me included. Much more so for the mothers of course".

Concerning child removal, Reginald McCaffrey, the Acting Director of Native Affairs in the Territory in the early 1950s, was, if anything, even more blunt. "The policy at the time I took over from Moy was you took the child from the breast of the mother and brought it to Darwin to be sent to either of one or two missions." This policy was quite "unnecessary". It "should never have happened". McCaffrey's interviewer was clearly surprised. Were the children really taken by force? "Yes. There were great scenes of gins screaming their lungs out ... Great scenes ... Post war they were taken off the breast forcibly." According to McCaffrey it was only by the time that Harry Giese took over the Welfare Branch in the mid 1950s that the "brakes" were applied on such a cruel policy.

Another Territory patrol officer was Jeremy Long. In 1967 he wrote an article for the anthropological journal *Oceania*. At that time, Long did not claim that children were removed because they were "outcasts" or because of ill-health or for the sake of education. This is what he wrote: "For some years it remained the practice to persuade the Aboriginal parents of 'half-caste' children to consent to the removal of such children to institutions without any real examination of the reasons for separating the child from its parents. It was repugnant to see an almost white child living among Aborigines and this was reason enough to remove the child." Eventually Jeremy Long wrote a history of the patrol officers in the Northern Territory entitled *The Go-Betweens*. In this history he pointed out that in 1950 the Government Secretary at Darwin, R. S. Leydin, had described the removal policy as likely not only to attract criticism for the "violation of the present-day conception of 'human rights'" but also "to outrage the feelings of the average observer". Long agreed with Dr Charles Duguid's description of Aboriginal child removal as the patrol officers' "most hated task".

Yet old men, it seems, forget. In the 1990s the removal policies in the Northern Territory finally became a major public issue, because of both *Bringing them home* and the legal action against the Commonwealth taken by Lorna Cubillo and Peter Gunner. In the early 1980s those who had once been responsible for removing the "half-caste" children had no difficulty in admitting to the terrible, pointless injustice of what had occurred. By contrast, in the late 1990s, other administrators of the child removal policy who were still alive, and who felt maligned and misunderstood by the authors of *Bringing them home*, found a highly receptive audience for the very different tale they now told.

One of the most influential of these witnesses from the past was the former cadet patrol officer Colin Macleod. Rarely in the history of public controversy in this country has so deep a trust been placed by so many with an interest in a matter of public importance in something so superficial and insubstantial as Macleod's memoir of his experiences as a patrol officer in the Northern Territory, *Patrol in the Dreamtime*.

In this memoir Macleod claimed that before his time "full blood" children were often taken from their families and cultures "for the purpose of their supposed better assimilation into our 'superior' way of life". No-one with any understanding of removal policy in the Territory has ever claimed that the policy involved "full blood" Aborigines. Macleod claimed that "it was the churches—not the Welfare Branch—that engaged in social engineering by removing Aboriginal children from their families for ideological—rather than pragmatic—reasons." This is wrong. Before the Second World War, as we have seen, the removal policy of Dr Cook was highly ideological. Moreover the child removal policy was always under the control of the government. Before 1939 the separated children were mainly sent to the state institutions in Darwin and Alice Springs. After 1939 the government continued to collect the children, to retain guardianship over them and to send them to the special-purpose Christian homes it supervised and subsidised.

In *Patrol in the Dreamtime* Macleod claimed that children were "never … taken from families with a mother and father". In fact very many removed children had close attachments to both Aboriginal mothers and fathers. Macleod gave evidence on behalf of the Commonwealth at the Cubillo–Gunner case. He was asked how he knew that children with mothers and fathers were never removed. "It's only a belief," he replied.

Macleod claimed that the children removed were "*always* [his italics] from very young and unprotected single mothers, often young girls between 10 and 13 with no family members to properly care for them". Always? In his own memoir Macleod discusses a report he made in November 1957 which recommended the removal of three girls. One was five, one was nine, one was eleven. All were daughters of the same Aboriginal mother, Elsie. Was a woman with an eleven-year-old child "very young"? In this very case his own generalisation is proven false. In his evidence to the Cubillo–Gunner case Macleod was asked how he knew that removals were invariably of children of very young mothers. Disarmingly, he replied that what he had written was perhaps not "absolutely correct".

And so it goes on. In *Patrol in the Dreamtime* Macleod discusses in some detail certain removal guidelines produced by Ted Milliken, an Assistant Director of Welfare who arrived in the Territory at much the same time as he did. They are reprinted as an appendix to *Patrol in the Dreamtime*. These guidelines, which are unusually sensitive to Aboriginal society, bear almost no relationship to the practice of "half-caste" child removal. In fact they were not produced by Milliken until 1959, well after Macleod had left the Territory for good. During the Cubillo–Gunner case Macleod was asked about these guidelines. He admitted he had never set eyes upon them until he began to write his book almost forty years later.

In *Patrol in the Dreamtime* Macleod writes with an assumed anthropological confidence about social and familial structures in the traditional Aboriginal world. "Full-blooded Aborigines and part-Aboriginals did not always see themselves as one people … [Young] girls did not always have a place in tribal society, so they ended up in limbo … The tribal husbands of the mothers of half-castes did not always recognise that child. Thus the child would have no protection nor be incorporated into the skin system." And so on. He was asked in the Cubillo–Gunner case whether he knew anything at all about the kinship system. "A little bit," he replied, "not a great deal." His modesty was not false. After two questions his knowledge of the kinship system was exhausted.

During the course of this cross-examination, Colin Macleod felt the need on a number of occasions to explain that his memoir was not "a treatise" and that it had to be remembered that he left the Territory more than forty years ago. Was he saying, then, he was asked, that the information in his book could not be relied upon? Macleod hardly resisted the thought. His memoir was "a cameo shot", the "recollections" of a "young boy".

Colin Macleod had been employed as a cadet patrol officer in his early twenties. He arrived in the Territory knowing nothing about Aborigines. He left the Territory after about three and a half years. Since then he had had no further contact with Aborigines. During his period as a cadet patrol officer he recommended the removal of children on one occasion only. He never saw a copy of the standard form used in the removal process, let alone removed an Aboriginal child while on patrol. And yet Macleod's views were given very great prominence by right-wing news-paper columnists and by key administrators of Aboriginal affairs. An extract from *Patrol in the Dreamtime* appeared as an appendix to the belated government submission on *Bringing them home*. On a number of occasions in that submission the government case relied on the authority of Colin Macleod. The Minister for Aboriginal Affairs, Senator Herron, was an admirer of *Patrol in the Dreamtime*. So, it is rumoured, was the Prime Minister, John Howard. Enemies of *Bringing them home* were highly critical of the anecdotal evidence of the 535 Aboriginal witnesses on which it supposedly relied. They had no difficulty, however, with the anecdotal evidence produced by one white patrol officer who had left the Territory more than forty years ago at the age of twenty-four. In truth Colin Macleod understood remarkably little about the history of Aboriginal child removal. Yet because he was singing a tune which many Australians wanted to hear, his opinions carried a very considerable and altogether undeserved weight.

At much the same time as Colin Macleod was appointed a cadet patrol officer in the Northern Territory, Reginald Marsh, a senior public servant in the Department of Territories, was posted to Darwin. He remained there for several years. Macleod believes that the main reason Aboriginal children were taken from their parents was to save the girls from becoming the sexual playthings of exploitative European men. In *Quadrant* magazine in June 1999 Reginald Marsh published an article, "'Lost', 'Stolen' or "Rescued"", which proposed a rather different case.

Marsh's theory about Aboriginal child removal went like this. The "genetic health" of traditional Aboriginal society rested upon strict conformity to a "changeless" law, and in particular upon what anthropologists had come to call the moiety system, namely the division of all Aboriginal clans into two separate groups and the total prohibition of marriage within the single group. According to Marsh this traditional order was threatened by contact with Europeans. Some children were now born as a result of the sexual union between the Aboriginal female and the European male. They represented something hitherto "unthinkable", a child without a link to both moieties. Such a child might be killed at birth. If it survived, it faced ostracism. In certain cases mothers might be able to raise their children by withdrawing from the traditional world. In other cases responsible Europeans who had fathered such children might solve the problem they posed by sending them away. In yet other cases it became the responsibility of the government, in the interests of the children, to save them from the "intolerable" situation in which they had been placed.

Marsh conceded that some mothers might have resented the removal of children they had suckled. He was convinced, however, that the Aboriginal society as a whole approved. The interests of the group predominated over the interest of the individual mother. Indeed he knew of "no evidence that any traditional community ever protested against the removal of a part-Aboriginal child". It was ridiculous to speak of "stolen" children. "Rescued" children would make more sense.

There is little doubt that Reginald Marsh in his *Quadrant* article presented a coherent theory about Aboriginal child removal. Is it, however, true?

There is, first of all, an important ambiguity in Marsh's case. Is he trying to explain the policy and practice of child removal in the Northern Territory or the phenomenon of child removal in the country as a whole? If the latter, his theory makes no sense. From the beginning of the twentieth century, Aboriginal children began to be removed systematically from their families and communities not only in the areas where traditional societies survived—the Northern Territory, Central Australia, the north of Western Australia—but also in the predominantly mixed descent areas of the southern States and the south of Western Australia where traditional law, including, of course, the moiety system, had long since broken down. Even in the early decades of the century the Aboriginal children who were taken from their parents under Donaldson's regime in New South Wales or Neville's in the south of Western Australia could not possibly have been removed for the reasons suggested by the theory of Reginald Marsh.

Might Marsh be right, however, with regard to child removals in those areas where traditional societies survived? Once more, it seems, not so. Over the past two years I have examined thousands of documents, buried in government archives, concerning the policy and practice of Aboriginal child removal in the Northern Territory and the States. In these documents the administrators provide a number of different justifications for the separation of Aboriginal children. It is frequently claimed that "half-caste" children must be removed in order to save them from the squalor and degradation of the primitive Aboriginal way of life. It is frequently said that children must be saved from a life of idleness and given a rudimentary education in order to prepare them for a place among the lower orders of the European world. Frequently the officials speak of the scandal of seeing "nearly white" children living among the blacks. On one or two occasions I have read accounts of "half-caste" children being removed from black camps in order to prevent their participation in an initiation ceremony. I cannot recall one occasion where the documentary evidence suggested that a child was removed on the grounds that the traditional law excluded them from full participation in the Aboriginal world. If "half-caste" children were removed for the kind of reason Marsh suggests, how is the silence of the documentary record to be explained?

Yet the problem with Marsh's article is deeper still. There is considerable evidence to suggest that he is quite wrong to assume that the smooth incorporation of the "half-caste" child or adult into traditional society was a theoretical impossibility. Marsh is an admirer of the patrol officer and popular writer Bill Harney, who lived among the Aborigines of the Northern Territory for much of his adult life. In one of his memoirs, *North of 23 Degrees*, Harney described a native camp at a station homestead "where, amidst laughter, swimming or maybe out hunting with their father or mother, these little half-castes would live among their own people, tended by all the tribe and particularly by a mother who watches over her child and tends to its wants". The anthropologist Kenneth Maddock was commissioned by the Commonwealth government, in the Cubillo–Gunner case, to investigate the question of whether or not "half-castes" were excluded from the traditional Aboriginal world. In the paper he wrote, although there are cases of ostracism, Maddock also cites numerous examples where anthropologists encountered "half-castes" fully initiated into the ceremonial life of the traditional world.

On one occasion A. E. Elkin came upon a young "half-caste" with a bull-thrower. This man, Elkin wrote, had "spent twenty-odd or thirty years amongst whites, and yet he was fully possessed by the emotions attached to this symbol of the secret life; and this was just as true of the other half-castes". Many years later another anthropologist, Diane Bell, found among the Pitjanjatjara women that children of mixed descent created only "minor problems". She found that the promised husbands of women with "half-caste" children took "responsibility for the children even to the extent of initiating and betrothing them in the customary manner". Maddock himself had worked among traditional Aborigines in the area of Katherine and the Beswick Reserve. "Some part-Aboriginal yellow-fellows", he had written, "have been brought up in the blackfellows' camps and are to all intents and purposes blackfellows themselves; they are brought up as within the pale of blackfellows' law and, if male, are admitted in the usual way to religious cults; I am unaware of Aboriginal prejudice against them on account of their mixed ancestry."

Aboriginal society was far more flexible, Aboriginal law far less changeless than Marsh allows. His theory of Aboriginal child removal is, accordingly, to a very large extent a myth.

There are other, no doubt smaller, problems with Reginald Marsh's contribution to the Aboriginal child removal debate. In his *Quadrant* article he was critical of the authors of *Bringing them home* for their "emotive" subtitle "Report on the Stolen Generation". No such subtitle exists. In his *Quadrant* article Marsh complained bitterly about the fact that he had not been "called" to give evidence before the Wilson–Dodson inquiry. In fact no witnesses who appeared before this inquiry were "called". All responded to newspaper advertisements. Reginald Marsh appeared at a *Quadrant* conference in August 1999, shortly after his article was published. The editor of *Quadrant*, P. P. McGuinness, reported on one of his interventions thus. Marsh "described … the absurdity of the notion of a policy of deliberate theft of children … In particular he referred to the history of Charles Perkins, whose mother had asked Mr Marsh to facilitate the education of Charles and his brothers." Really? Charles Perkins was sent, with the consent of his mother, from Alice Springs to Adelaide in 1945. Reginald Marsh first arrived in Darwin nine years later, in 1954. By the time he had reached Darwin Perkins was out of school and eighteen years of age.

In the issue of *Quadrant* where Reginald Marsh's article appeared, a long-retired Liberal politician, Peter Howson, published a companion piece, "Rescued from the Rabbit Burrow". Howson was in fact one of the most energetic campaigners against *Bringing them home* and the idea of the stolen generations. In the course of this campaign, apart from his *Quadrant* contributions, he wrote newspaper articles for the *Age*, the *Sydney Morning Herald* and the *Herald-Sun* and appeared as a witness before the Senate inquiry into the adequacy of the Howard government's response to the recommendations of *Bringing them home*. At this inquiry Howson claimed to have read the entire 8,000 pages of evidence given during the course of the Cubillo–Gunner case. He presented to it an extraordinary submission. Concerning the question of the stolen generations Peter Howson was obsessed.

Why? Australian journalists have taken remarkably little interest in the informal ideological groupings that help determine their country's life.

Howson is in fact a member of a Melbourne right-wing fraternity that includes such people as the former Treasury officials John Stone and Des Moore and the *éminence noire* of the ideological right in Australia, Ray Evans, the speech writer for the Chief Executive of Western Mining, Hugh Morgan. The Stone–Evans group has been very influential in Australian politics over the past twenty years. During the 1980s, through the H. R. Nicholls Society, it led the campaign against trade union power. In 1990 it helped launch Peter Costello and David Kemp on their political careers. During the 1990s the Stone-Evans group extended its interests beyond free market economics to constitutional conservatism (the Samuel Griffith Society) and Aboriginal affairs. Members campaigned, first against *Mabo* and native title, and then, after 1997, against *Bringing them home*.

Peter Howson, a conservative Christian member of the Stone–Evans group, was from 1955 to 1972 a Liberal Party member for an outer sub-urban Melbourne seat; from 1971 to 1972 he was the Minister responsible for Aboriginal affairs in the McMahon government. In this role he proved himself an orthodox supporter of the once bipartisan policy of Aboriginal assimilation, whose chief architect was Menzies' Minister for Territories, Paul Hasluck. Howson was given the Aboriginal portfolio at one of the nation's turning points, when the policy of assimilation was giving way to a new policy of land rights, self-determination and acknowledgment of the great injustice of Australian history, Aboriginal dispossession. Howson, as responsible minister, could neither sympathise with nor, in truth, understand the winds of change. His thinking as minister is recorded in great detail in the political diary he published with Penguin Books, and analysed astutely by Tim Rowse in *Obliged To Be Difficult*, his monograph on Nugget Coombs and indigenous affairs. As Minister, Howson was an increasingly fearful and bitter opponent of "black power", land rights and the Aboriginal Tent Embassy which was erected in front of the Federal Parliament. He became increasingly suspicious of his Prime Minister, William McMahon, who for opportunistic reasons, as Howson interpreted it, flirted with the anti-assimilationists on the government advisory body, the Council for Aboriginal Affairs. He gravitated naturally towards the true reactionaries in Aboriginal affairs, like Queensland Premier Joh Bjelke-Petersen. In the struggles over Aboriginal politics his most formidable enemy was the public servant Nugget Coombs.

Coombs was one of the dominant intellectual forces in the early 1970s sea change in Aboriginal affairs. He was also a skilled operator in the corridors of power. At first Howson thought he had merely been outmanoeuvred by Coombs. Gradually he came to see that Coombs's victory over him represented something much broader—a paradigm shift in Aboriginal politics in this country. Howson never forgave Coombs. He seems destined to wrestle with the ghost of Nugget Coombs for the remainder of his life.

In 1996 Howson wrote the preface to a book written by the right-wing Adelaide academic Geoffrey Partington praising Sir Paul Hasluck and attacking Nugget Coombs. The book was launched by the new Minister for Aboriginal Affairs in the Howard Government, Senator John Herron. "The evidence in this book shows", Howson wrote, "that [the] tragic state of contemporary Australian Aboriginal society is in large measure due to the abandonment of Hasluckian policies of unforced assimilation, patiently pursued with steady success from 1950 until 1968, and the introduction of policies of Aboriginal separation, which H. C. Coombs was able to persuade a succession of governments to adopt from 1968 onwards." This sentence expressed, in a nutshell, the standard Howson line.

Shortly after Howson wrote this preface, Bringing them home was published. It was, of course, critical of both Hasluck and assimilation. For Peter Howson the thirty years struggle with the old foe, who had once undone him, now resumed.

Howson's first serious intervention in the anti-Bringing them home campaign was the Quadrant article "Rescued from a Rabbit Burrow". It began strangely. In the late 1940s, Howson reminded us, one of the great symbolic encounters of the Cold War had occurred: the martyr of the left Alger Hiss had been convicted of perjury because of certain microfilmed documents a former agent of the communist underground, Whittaker Chambers, had secreted in a pumpkin. A few months before Chambers hid his microfilm at Utopia Station, Howson continued, Peter Gunner, one of the plaintiffs in the stolen generations' first case, had been born. According to the Commonwealth's barristers Gunner had been abandoned in a rabbit burrow by his mother and left to die. "The rabbit hole may now become, for Australia," Howson argued, "what the pumpkin and its content symbolised in the United States fifty years ago."

Howson's argument astonished me. The confrontation between Alger Hiss and Whittaker Chambers served as a symbol of the Cold War struggle between two rival political systems and ideologies, one of which, Stalinism, was responsible for the deaths of millions of innocent human beings and the subjugation of all of Europe east of the River Elbe. The case of Peter Gunner against the Commonwealth served as a symbol for the struggle over what to make of Aboriginal child removal or, more generally, the treatment of Aborigines after the nineteenth-century dispossession. The left-wing supporters of Alger Hiss did not see the evil that Stalinism was. The supporters of Peter Gunner, on the other hand, believed that it had been wrong and often racist for government officials to take Aboriginal children from their mothers without informed consent or reference to a court. Was Howson really unbalanced enough to believe that sympathy for the suffering of the stolen generations was the equivalent of progressivist blindness to the evil of Stalinism fifty years before?

As it turned out, Howson's rabbit burrow triumphalism was premature. Although in the Gunner case the Commonwealth brought evidence that suggested Peter Gunner had himself once believed that his mother had abandoned him at birth, it was never able to overcome the fact that its most important source for the story of attempted infanticide—Dora McLeod, the wife of the owner of Utopia Station—had failed to make mention of the abandonment of Peter Gunner either in her detailed diary or in the rather dotty evidence she presented to the court. In his judgment Justice O'Loughlin found that the story of the attempted infanticide of Gunner could not be proved. Even more importantly, he found that at the time Peter Gunner was taken by government officials he was a happy and a healthy seven year old, who was fully accepted as a member of the Aboriginal community at Utopia. The *Quadrant* attempt to make the rabbit burrow a symbol of the stolen generations hoax was not only tasteless and offensive; it had fallen rather flat.

In the remainder of his article what Howson had to say about the stolen generations was either derivative or downright false. In somewhat cruder form, Howson repeated the assertions of Reginald Marsh about the "tragic" incapacity of part-Aborigines to find a place in a primitive society where "genealogy is everything". For someone who was obsessed by *Bringing them home* Howson proved himself remarkably ill-informed about it. He called the inquiry into child removal a Royal Commission. It was no such thing. This was not a trivial mistake. Howson frequently criticised the Wilson–Dodson inquiry for its failure "to call" as witnesses missionaries, policemen or patrol officers. As a former Minister surely he should have understood that while Royal Commissions have *subpoena* powers, ordinary commissions of inquiry do not. The supposed failure of Sir Ronald Wilson and Mick Dodson "to call" certain witnesses was destined to become one of the great canards of the anti-*Bringing them home* campaign.

For the rest Howson's article merely regurgitated his standard line. Coombs's policy of "separation" has been an unmitigated disaster for the Aborigines. Aborigines had no alternative but to abandon fantasies of a return to the life of hunter–gatherers and to "get a life" inside the modern world. Coombsian policies were not only harming Aborigines, but the Australian national interest as well. By granting Aborigines land rights, and turning them into "rent seekers" with consultation rights, many promising mining projects had been put at risk. By speaking of Aboriginal injustice, Australia's good name was being sullied by new-class intellectuals driven by a pathological hatred for "the values and achievements of western civilisation". In Howson's strange world view the connection between sympathy for the stolen generations and treachery to Australia was clear.

In May 2000 Peter Howson wrote a submission on the question of the stolen generations issue to a Senate inquiry. Its contents deserve to be more widely known. Howson argued here not only that "almost all" Aboriginal child removals were "legally and morally justified" but also that those who believed otherwise had fallen prey to the Rousseauian myth of the noble savage, that is to say "of the idyllic, prelapsarian nature of the warm, generous and loving society, living harmoniously with nature, from which these children were brutally kidnapped". According to Howson the reality was very different. "It takes very little research to reach the conclusion that prior to 1788 Australia's aborigines were on the brink of extinction." And not only that. According to Howson, before the British arrived life in Aboriginal society was so unrelievedly bleak and horrible that it could best be characterised in the words used by Thomas Hobbes to describe the life of man not in society but in the state of nature, namely "solitary, poor, nasty, brutish and short". According to Howson, when the Christian missions arrived the Aborigines "discovered that these places provided sanctuary from brutality and sudden death ... and the inestimable benefits of civilisation". "It is no accident", he concluded, "that those who suffered most in this condition of life, particularly the women, seized the opportunity to escape from it when, miraculously, missionaries and pastoralists turned up and offered sanctuary. If the women had most to gain from the new life on offer, the men were not far behind."

According to Howson, then, as soon as the missionaries and pastoralists arrived, Aborigines fled as refugees from their own barbarous world, which vicious inter-tribal war had brought to the edge of extinction— after 40,000 years! Concerning the Aborigines Australia has nothing to apologise for. It is not only the "rescued" children of mixed descent but the Aboriginal people as a whole who ought to express gratitude for their miraculous deliverance from the Hobbesian hell of their own creation which occurred when the British, at long last, arrived on Australian shores.

It is a sobering thought that racist nonsense of this kind was written not by an obscure and isolated crank but by a frequently published former Australian government minister who had once held responsibility for Aboriginal affairs.

THE GENERAL

In cultural politics every campaign is well served by the presence of a general. In the anti-*Bringing them home* campaign, the general was undoubtedly P. P. McGuinness, the *Sydney Morning Herald* opinion columnist and *Quadrant* editor.

McGuinness was appointed to *Quadrant* after I resigned the editorship in November 1997. Technically my resignation was triggered by the unwillingness of the old guard on the *Quadrant* Board of Management, Dame Leonie Kramer and Professor David Armstrong, to offer support when Les Murray, *Quadrant*'s literary editor, began to conduct, in his own words, a "feud" against me. In fact the resignation was more a consequence of the bad blood caused by articles and editorials written in 1996 and 1997 by myself and a close friend, Raimond Gaita, on Aboriginal politics in general and the question of genocide and the stolen generations in particular. In the letter Les Murray sent me in June 1997, which convinced me that our working relations were at an end, Murray wrote that he regarded as my "most serious" failure my behaviour on "the Aboriginal front". According to Murray, I had started to take "the received leftist line on Aborigines … letting the man Gaita trumpet against dissent on this matter. I began to wonder, if the Melbourne left succeeded in duchessing you and getting you to bring *Quadrant* over to them, where voices on this matter not as yet howled down by the claques, voices like say Geoffrey Partington, might hope for a platform." Nor was Murray alone. At the

November 1997 meeting of the *Quadrant* Committee of Management, where I resigned, the criticism from the Kramer–Armstrong old guard was dominated by discussion of *Quadrant* and the Aborigines.

In the last issue of *Quadrant* I edited, I published as my parting shot a long essay on the stolen generations. In the same issue the newly appointed editor, P. P. McGuinness, made clear the new direction the magazine would take. He intended, he wrote, to discard the "mawkish sentimentality" that had overtaken discussions concerning the Aborigines in recent years. While McGuinness promised "genuine debate" on the stolen generations and *Bringing them home*, he was also very critical of the report, characterising its call for an apology to the "stolen children" as "pharasaical breast beating" and even as an attempt at "thought control". At the time I wondered whether characterising those with whom McGuinness disagreed as mawkish sentimentalists and totalitarian thought police was the best way to encourage "genuine debate".

My scepticism was not misplaced. Over the next three years *Quadrant* became devoted to ever wilder and more extreme attacks on every cause and belief of the contemporary Aboriginal political leadership and its support base. In March 1998 *Quadrant* published a highly personal attack on Sir Ronald Wilson by Rosemary O'Grady which argued, absurdly enough, that Sir Ronald's sympathy for the stolen generations was in fact a cover for his indifference to Aboriginal land rights. In May it published Ron Brunton's article on genocide and the "unconceived generations" which I have already discussed, and in September a characteristically supercilious article by the political philosopher Kenneth Minogue, which interpreted concerns about historic injustice to the Aborigines as nothing more than the display of moral vanity by the intellectual class; which argued that the sorrow expressed after the publication of *Bringing them home* showed only that Australians "have mastered the art of public sentimentality as pioneered in the grief for the death of Princess Diana"; which sagely reminded us all that "from the no doubt limited perspective of the surfer on the beach the Aborigines are a pretty incompetent lot"; and which came to the interesting conclusion that, concerning the separation of Aboriginal children, no alternative policy was even "plausible". Apparently, at least where Aborigines were concerned, the idea of leaving babies and children with their mothers except in cases of proven neglect had not occurred to the Oakeshottian Minogue, normally an opponent of the interventionist "nanny state".

And so, at an accelerating pace, it went on. In 1999 and the first half of 2000 Quadrant published the "rescued children" contributions by Reginald Marsh and Peter Howson; an article by the former Labor Minister Gary Johns, advising Quadrant readers that when it came to reconciliation they should "read the fine print"; two articles hostile to the idea of land rights in the Northern Territory; another article by Ron Brunton, this time on "Hindmarsh Island and the Hoaxing of Aboriginal Anthropology"; and yet another article by Peter Howson, with his Chicken Little theme about the sky having fallen in since the age of Nugget Coombs.

All this, however, was nothing compared with what was to come. In the final four issues of Quadrant in 2000, McGuinness published an article by Geoffrey Partington on the failure of Aboriginal education; an article by Keith Windschuttle concerning the supposed "Break-up of Australia" that was to come as a result of the "separatist" thinking in the work of Henry Reynolds and Nugget Coombs; no fewer than five long articles— by Douglas Meagher QC, David Bennett QC, Professor Kenneth Maddock, Ron Brunton and John McDonnell—celebrating from different angles the Commonwealth victory in the Cubillo–Gunner stolen generations test case; and, most astonishingly of all, three lengthy articles by Keith Windschuttle supposedly exploding the left-wing "myth" of the nineteenth-century frontier massacres and its "manufacture of a vastly inflated death toll".

Within three years under the editorship of P. P. McGuinness Quadrant had moved from the promise of "genuine debate" on Aboriginal policy to the reality of atrocity denialism in the David Irving mode. No doubt

Leonie Kramer, David Armstrong and Les Murray (whose biographer, Peter Alexander has been hoodwinked into believing that his subject is a political friend of Mick and Patrick Dodson) are pleased.

In the course of the *Quadrant* campaign on the Aboriginal front McGuinness contributed no original ideas of his own. He did, however, publish one long editorial on the issue of Aboriginal child removal— "Poor Fella My 'Stolen Generation'"—for the November issue of 1999. As an example of what passes for serious intellectual commentary among the members of the contemporary right in Australia this editorial is worth examination in some detail.

It begins like this: "Were there any 'stolen children', in the sense of Aboriginal children taken away against the will of their parents or their mother? Undoubtedly there were." Any? On the basis of a 1994 survey by the Australian Bureau of Statistics, which McGuinness had once praised highly in the *Sydney Morning Herald*, we know that about 10% of Aboriginal children, between 20,000 and 25,000 in number, were separated from both parents in the decades before 1970. We know, on the basis of the historical chapters in *Bringing them home*, that in New South Wales before 1940, in Western Australia before 1951 and in the Northern Territory before 1953, these children were, according to the relevant laws, removed by the authorities without the need for parental consent or the requirement that the authorities prove neglect before a court. We also know that before the 1970s, in every Australian State, Aboriginal children charged with neglect under general legislation were removed from parents who had neither legal representation nor even the remotest understanding of their legal rights. Were there "any" stolen children, then? Of course there were— very many thousands.

McGuinness's editorial continues: "Were there any massacres by whites of Aborigines? Yes, we know for example that at Myall Creek in 1838 there were an estimated twenty-eight Aborigines slaughtered by a party of squatters and their employees, and we also know that seven of the whites were hanged for the murders." Once again, both McGuinness's question and his answer are misleading in the extreme. Australian historians have uncovered hundreds of sites where nineteenth-century frontier massacres of Aborigines occurred. In a meticulous study of Western Victoria, *Scars in the Landscape*, Ian Clark found evidence of no fewer than 107 killing sites, ranging from places where one or two Aborigines had been slaughtered to places where dozens had been put to death. Because killing Aborigines was, technically at least, a serious crime, it seems highly likely that many massacres went unrecorded. Nor is there any reason to believe the death toll in Western Victoria exceptional. Almost all historians agree that killings in Queensland, where according to the careful research of Henry Reynolds and Noel Loos 850 non-Aborigines lost their lives, were worse than elsewhere in Australia. In his pioneering work *Invasion and Resistance* (1982), Noel Loos conducted a painstaking investigation into the frontier killings in the north of Queensland. As he points out, Aborigines were shot even for disturbing or killing cattle, let alone for killing settlers, and were subject to the raids of the Queensland Native Police for almost half a century. He arrived at the conclusion that the slaughter of 4,000 Aborigines in the north of Queensland, and 8,500 in Queensland as a whole, were estimates "so conservative as to be misleading". To write, as McGuinness does, as if there is a serious question about whether "any" frontier massacres took place in nineteenth-century Australia is absurd.

And not only that. So far as I can tell Myall Creek was the only occasion during the entire history of the nineteenth-century frontier massacres when perpetrators were found guilty of murder. In a small number of other cases massacres were investigated but legal proceedings dropped. In an even smaller number Europeans were brought to trial but either found not guilty or guilty of less serious offences, like causing grievous bodily harm. In the overwhelming majority of cases where Aborigines were massacred no official investigation took place. To imply, as McGuinness does, that the resolution of the Myall Creek massacre was typical, or to suggest, as he does later in his editorial, that it reveals the underlying strength of "British justice" and "the rule of law in New South Wales" with regard to the Aborigines, is altogether false.

"Were there", McGuinness continues, "any cases of poisoned flour being given to the Aborigines with the intention of killing them? Perhaps, but it is hard to pin down a documented example." In the absence of any documented case, he writes later in the editorial, the "poisoned flour" furphy is best regarded as "the rural version of an urban myth". Really?

During the course of the nineteenth century there were dozens of accounts by settlers that told of Aborigines dying after eating flour poisoned either by arsenic or strychnine which had been left by farmers or shepherds as bait. In his study of atrocities against Aborigines on the Queensland frontier, the historian Raymond Evans cites accounts by settlers of the poisoning of Aborigines—near Laidley; at Whitesides and Apis Stations; at Rush Creek and Cardwell Districts. Evans quotes E. W. Docker of North Queensland who called poisoning Aborigines "almost a common occurrence" and the Reverend Campion who was told: "If you give the blacks phosphorous in their flour it only makes their eyes water, but if you mix arsenic with the flour, that'll stretch them out." He also quotes the eyewitness account, by an old Aborigine, of the notorious poisoning of large numbers of Aborigines at Kilroy Creek in 1842.

Certain cases of poisoning are well documented. In *Scars in the Landscape*, for example, Ian Clark tells the story of a number of poisonings of Aborigines reported to have taken place at the station of Dr James Kilgour, near Port Fairy in Victoria. Initial investigations were conducted by Dr John Walton. In October 1842 he conveyed his findings to the Port Phillip Protector, George Augustus Robinson, in the following words: "It appears that the then overseer ... had sent away into the bush to some natives ... a quantity of what was supposed to be flour. Of this they partook, and were immediately seized with burning pains in the stomach, vomiting, sinking of the abdomen and intense thirst (which are the symptoms produced by arsenic); on the following morning three men, three women and three children were dead." Because the bodies of the victims were burned and no white witnesses could be found, charges could not be laid. Six months later George Augustus Robinson visited Port Fairy. He heard how six Aborigines had been unable to walk since being poisoned. He visited their campsite at Tarrone and saw their affliction with his own eyes. The evidence suggested that one of James Kilgour's employees, a shepherd called Robertson, had administered the poison. In 1844 Kilgour was advised that his station licence would only be renewed if he resided on the station himself or employed a morally suitable manager.

Three years later an even better documented example of murder by poison occurred at Kangaroo Creek near the Clarence River in New South Wales. Its story has been told by Jane Lydon in the journal *Aboriginal History*. Here four Europeans testified to the poisoning on 28 November 1847 of some twenty-three Aborigines. They named as the culprit the pastoralist Thomas Coutts. A Crown Commissioner, Oliver Fry, was convinced of Coutts's guilt. He regarded the case as "one of the most hideous enormities that has ever taken place in any age or country". Coutts was arrested and committed for trial. On 8 May 1848, however, the New South Wales Attorney-General, John Plunkett, the man who had been responsible for bringing the Myall Creek murderers to justice, decided not to proceed with the case. Plunkett was in no "moral doubt" about the overwhelming likelihood of Coutts's "guilt of the dreadful crime". His problem was that under British law at that time Aborigines were not thought to be capable of taking an oath and, therefore, of being fit to testify. Plunkett believed that in the absence of Aboriginal eyewitnesses to the poisoning the chances of a successful prosecution were very poor.

If, then, there were no cases in which Europeans were found guilty of poisoning Aborigines, it was essentially because of the obstacles even the few humane and determined officials, such as Plunkett and Robinson, had to overcome before bringing such cases to trial. It is the combination of these legal difficulties with McGuinness's ignorance of the historical record that gives him the confidence to pronounce the murder of Aborigines by use of poisoned flour a rural myth.

The first paragraph of McGuinness's "Poor Fella" editorial concludes with this argument: "Did some bureaucrats in areas of policy-making advocate the steady disappearance of Aborigines by assimilation of mixed bloods and the inevitable disappearance of full-blooded Aborigines attached to their own culture and way of life? Yes, there is clear evidence of that. But was this the basis for policy in any specific State or Territory …? Is there any Government policy statement, or internal policy document, as distinct from views expressed by individual bureaucrats however senior, to this effect? No-one has found one." Here McGuinness has returned from atrocities in general to the specific issue of the stolen generations. Once more he is completely wrong, as the following brief analysis reveals.

During the inter-war period the Commonwealth government was responsible for Aboriginal administration in the Northern Territory. Its most important official in the field was the Chief Protector of Aborigines. Between 1927 and 1939 the Chief Protector in the Territory was Dr Cecil Cook. He was, as we have seen, the advocate of a policy of collecting "half-caste" children in institutions with the ultimate purpose of arranging for their biological absorption into the European population through a racial eugenics program he called "breeding out the colour". McGuinness seems to think this project represented merely the private views of Cook. He denies—on what basis I do not know—that the Commonwealth government ever gave the policy its support. But was this so?

On 7 February 1933 Dr Cook sent the following memorandum to his superior in the Department of the Interior in Canberra: "Every endeavour is being made to breed out the colour by elevating female half-castes to white standard with a view to their absorption by mating into the white population. The adoption of a similar policy throughout the Commonwealth is, in my opinion, a matter of vital importance." The officials in Canberra and their Minister, J. A. Perkins, gave support to Cook's proposal for an extension of the Territory policy to Australia as a whole. The Secretary in the Department of the Interior, J. A. Carrodus, composed a memorandum of his own. "The policy of mating half-castes with whites, for the purpose of breeding out the colour, is that adopted by the Commonwealth government on the recommendation of Dr Cook." Carrodus suggested that although "unanimity might be difficult in regard to the matter … the subject might profitably be referred for discussion at a conference of Premiers". Carrodus's Minister, Perkins, agreed. The Department of the Prime Minister was approached. On 3 March 1933 it agreed to place the issue of an all-Australian policy of "breeding out the colour" on the agenda of the forthcoming Premiers' Conference. In preparation for this conference, on 29 May 1933 the Prime Minister's Department produced an official memorandum that defined Commonwealth government policy as the encouragement of "the marriage of half-castes with whites or half-castes, the object being to 'breed out' the colour as far as possible".

As it happened, the proposal never made it to the Premiers' Conference. Most likely the Chief Protector of Queensland, J. W. Bleakley, a conservative opponent of miscegenation, was the stumbling block. Nonetheless the policy of breeding out the colour received the full endorsement of the Commonwealth for at least another five years (and, for that matter, of the government in Western Australia during the same years). In 1938 Canberra corresponded with the Union of South Africa on the question of racial intermarriage. In December Carrodus forwarded to Pretoria a memorandum Cook had written in 1933 explaining in detail the policy of "breeding out the colour". Carrodus informed Pretoria that in the Northern Territory Cook's policy still applied.

McGuinness's contention that the policy of "breeding out the colour" was never "the basis for policy in any specific State or Territory", and his pronouncement that "no-one" had ever found a "government policy or even an internal policy document" to show that it was, are both completely wrong.

In his "Poor Fella" editorial McGuinness generally repeated the arguments already advanced in the anti-*Bringing them home* campaign. He added only one idea that was, almost, his own. Drawing on a suggestion first made by Ron Brunton, McGuinness argued here that the several hundreds of Aboriginal witnesses who had given evidence before the Wilson–Dodson inquiry, and presumably also the thousands of other separated children and their families who had not, might all, as part of some "collective hysteria", be suffering from the condition known as "false memory syndrome". McGuinness likened the testimony of the separated children to invented tales of childhood sexual abuse, Satanic possession or alien abduction. Was it not all too easy for "pedlars of quackery" to "implant" in Aboriginal minds the idea that their "awful" lives were the fault of wicked "outsiders" rather than their own "neglectful parents?"

"Slander", as Alexander Solzhenitsyn once said, "is a hummable tune." Despite the fact that McGuinness provided no evidence for his astonishing claim nor even defined what he meant by "false memory syndrome"—were the Aborigines who claimed to be members of the stolen generations fantasising about having been separated from their parents or only about the suffering of their childhood years?—his idea was destined to be enthusiastically embraced by the anti-*Bringing them home* campaigners. In April 2000 the publisher and journalist Michael Duffy wrote in the London *Spectator* of the "brave commentator" who had compared the stories of the stolen generations "with the failure of memory that occurs in cases such as people wrongly claiming childhood sexual assault or abduction by aliens". In October 2000, no less a figure than the former Governor-General Bill Hayden argued in a speech given nation-wide coverage that the conclusions of *Bringing them home* were "very much based" on something he called "faulty [sic] memory syndrome". Perhaps Mr Hayden was having memory problems of his own.

THE TROOPS

The campaign against *Bringing them home* and the idea of the stolen generations might not have had much influence if it had been conducted exclusively by right-wing think-tanks and in right-wing magazines. It became important largely because of the enthusiastic participation of certain opinion columnists in both the quality and the popular press— McGuinness himself in the *Sydney Morning Herald*, Frank Devine in the *Australian*, Christopher Pearson in the *Australian Financial Review*, Andrew Bolt in the *Herald-Sun* in Melbourne; Piers Akerman and Michael Duffy in what is probably the most influential newspaper with regard to public opinion in Australia today, Sydney's *Daily Telegraph*. These journalists invented no new arguments and uncovered no new facts. What they did, however, was make the main lines of the anti-*Bringing them home* campaign available to the general public and create, in regard to the idea that very many thousands of Aboriginal children had been removed from their families unjustly and for racist reasons, scepticism or outright disbelief.

The campaign, as it gained momentum in the daily press through the writings of these journalists, went roughly like this. The "half-caste" Aboriginal children who had been removed by governments over the course of the twentieth century had not been "stolen" but, as Reginald Marsh and Peter Howson had claimed in *Quadrant*, "rescued" from a traditional society in which, if they survived the threat of infanticide at birth, they became abused outcasts. "It needs to be stressed", Christopher Pearson pointed out, "that, from a traditional perspective, children with a non-Aboriginal parent had no place in the scheme of things." (*Australian Financial Review* 29/5/2000) Was it not typical of the "sorry industry", Piers Akerman argued, that they could not admit that even now "there can be no place in tribal law for so-called yeller-fellers"? (*Daily Telegraph* 4/4/2000) P. P. McGuinness, the publisher of Howson and Marsh, was outraged when a fellow journalist accused him of propagating the myth of the "rescued generations". This was, he wrote, "pure invention ... I have never, ever used the word 'rescue' or 'rescued' in my newspaper writing in connection with Aboriginal issues." (*Sydney Morning Herald* 27/5/2000) Never ever? In the *Sydney Morning Herald* of 10 January 1998 McGuinness explained Aboriginal child removal like this: "In many, if not all, cases it was a policy of rescuing children of mixed blood who were not likely to become full members of a tribe not having the proper 'skins', from marginalisation and abuse by tribal Aborigines." Far from never, ever referring to rescued children, McGuinness, as editor of *Quadrant*, was largely responsible for creating the myth of the "rescued generations". Apparently it did not occur to him, or to anyone else involved in the anti-*Bringing them home* campaign, that the majority of Aboriginal children removed from their parents came not from "tribal" situations in the Northern Territory or the north of Western Australia but from the mixed descent communities of New South Wales, Victoria and the southern parts of South Australia and Western Australia, where traditional law had altogether broken down and where, accordingly, the "rescued generations" argument was not only false but self-evidently so.

Sometimes different arguments about the motives of the child removers were suggested. Piers Akerman regretted the passing of that generation of Australians "who believed that young Aboriginal people would have a better chance of living a healthy, rewarding and fulfilling life if they were removed from the unhealthy humpy dwellings that used to cluster on the outskirts of rural settlements". (*Daily Telegraph* 27/1/1998) He claimed, moreover, that throughout twentieth-century Australia Aboriginal children could only be removed from their parents in cases where neglect had been proved before a court. He was, for example, bitterly contemptuous of the Boyer Lecturer Inga Clendinnen for "ignoring the reality that the removal of Aboriginal or part-Aboriginal children from their homes was covered by legal process in all the states and required court approval". (*Daily Telegraph* 16/12/1999) Piers Akerman abused the authors of *Bringing them home* in the most vicious and extravagant language, time and time again. If he had bothered to read the report he vilified, however, he would have discovered that the health and material well-being of the separated children was certainly no better and probably marginally worse than that of the children who had not been removed; and that, in regard to the Northern Territory, Western Australia, Queensland and New South Wales, for a considerable part of the twentieth century Aboriginal children could be taken from their parents without any need to refer the matter to a court. Clearly Akerman was telling his *Daily Telegraph* readership not the truth but what many wished to hear.

So, for a slightly different audience, was Christopher Pearson. On 8 March 1999 he informed the readers of the *Financial Review*, in discussing the Lorna Cubillo case, that the removal of Aboriginal children involved "basic social welfare interventions" which had nothing whatever to do with questions of race. Lorna Cubillo's mother was a "camp follower" of two nearby Phillip Creek army bases. Lorna herself was "at risk of being raped by soldiers and of being prostituted". That was why she had to be taken away. "The State", he claimed, "continues to remove children from mothers who attempt infanticide and from impoverished call-girls … and rightly so."

There were so many factual errors and conceptual confusions in Pearson's account that to unravel them takes time. To prove his claim that Aboriginal child removals were of a conventional social welfare kind, Pearson argued that Lorna Cubillo was removed because she was in danger of being raped by soldiers in the vicinity of Phillip Creek. From Phillip Creek, however, only "half-caste" children were removed, both boys and girls. Does Pearson believe, then, that the "full bloods" were not in danger of being raped, or that the "half-caste" boys were? The racial thinking behind the removal of Lorna Cubillo is clear. And anyhow, from where precisely did the danger to Lorna arise? According to the evidence of Les Penhall, the patrol officer who removed Lorna Cubillo in 1947, the army camps near Phillip Creek were closed at the end of the Second World War. If Lorna was in danger it was not from soldiers but from two of the missionaries in whose care she had been placed by the state. Some time after Lorna Cubillo was removed, a missionary–teacher at Phillip Creek called Thomas was sent to prison for the sexual abuse of children under his care. Lorna herself was savagely beaten and sexually frightened by another male missionary, this time at the Retta Dixon "half-caste" Home in Darwin where she was taken. Moreover, the evidence in the Cubillo case revealed that at Phillip Creek Lorna was surrounded by a loving extended family and community.

By what right does Pearson describe her as a neglected child or an outcast? By what right does he label her "mother"—in fact her mother's sister; her biological mother had died shortly after her birth—a "call girl"? (*Australian Financial Review* 8/3/1999) The abuse by the pompous and the privileged of the powerless and the dispossessed is not a pretty sight.

If the overwhelming majority of the separated Aboriginal children had been rescued from tribal exclusion or parental neglect, why was it being put about that they were "stolen"? Here the right-wing campaign spoke in a single voice—the "loose and hazy", "threadbare", "scandalous", "malevolent", "moralistic" Sir Ronald Wilson "propaganda forum" was to blame. In one of his opinion columns McGuinness bemoaned the hostility of the left to what he called a "nuanced discussion" of the question of the stolen generations. His own contribution to such a nuanced discussion was to label *Bringing them home* "a Big Lie". In general the attack on the Wilson–Dodson inquiry proceeded through repetitive abuse rather than analysis. Insofar as any arguments were provided to justify the attack, they followed Brunton's initial methodological critique, even at its most absurd. Both Frank Devine and Padraic McGuinness, for example, flailed the authors of *Bringing them home* for their failure to quote verbatim extracts from all the 535 Aboriginal witnesses it had heard. (*Sydney Morning Herald* 5/3/1998; *Australian* 5/3/1998)

According to the campaign, the man who had to shoulder most of the responsibility for the failures of *Bringing them home* was the co-chair of the inquiry, Sir Ronald Wilson. The extremity and the persistence of the attack on Wilson—one of the most humane and self-effacing Australians I have ever met—has to be read to be believed. Because Wilson was once a Presbyterian elder who had sat on the board of the Perth "quarter-caste" home, Sister Kate's, he was accused, according to the line first floated by Ron Brunton, of gross moral hypocrisy and even of harbouring a secret agenda to defend the financial interests of the Uniting Church. Wilson was at first criticised merely for "failing to call" potential defenders of the child removal policy—public servants, patrol officers, missionaries—to give evidence. It was not long, however, before other journalists followed the lead of Piers Akerman in accusing him, altogether falsely, of "barring" or "excluding" such witnesses "entirely". (*Daily Telegraph* 13/1/1998; *Australian* 11/9/2000) No evidence for this accusation was produced.

Sir Ronald Wilson was seen as the exemplar of that kind of Australian whose besetting sin was what Christopher Pearson called "moral vanity". (*Australian Financial Review* 17/1/2000) He was christened by Michael Duffy "Sir Ronald the Evangelist" and depicted as a modern-day missionary whose secret purpose was "to keep the blacks in their place". "The time has come to recognise", Duffy told his *Daily Telegraph* readers, that Wilson and those like him were "not the liberators of Aboriginal people but just their latest oppressors". (*Daily Telegraph* 12/8/2000) Frank Devine was at first offended by the *ad hominem* nature of Ron Brunton's attack on Sir Ronald Wilson. (*Australian* 5/3/1998) In September 2000, however, he supported the campaign characterisation of Wilson as a "distributor of malevolent myth". (*Australian* 11/9/2000) Over time the targets of the campaign extended to other "serial apologists" (Piers Akerman's term, *Daily Telegraph* 23/5/2000) like Sir William Deane ("Holy Billy") or Malcolm Fraser ("the sanctimonious prig"). (Akerman, *Daily Telegraph* 29/8/2000) Like Sir Ronald Wilson they were seen as betrayers of their race and class. Even though Mick Dodson had co-chaired the stolen generations inquiry, as an Aborigine he was assumed irrelevant to its work and outcome and was, thus, barely visible to the right-wing gaze.

How had *Bringing them home* come to wield such influence? The campaigners generally agreed with Andrew Bolt's suggestion that Australia was in the grip of a politically correct "moral mafia" who were determined to "strangle debate". (*Herald-Sun* 13/4/2000) Bolt thought the idea that Australia had a racist let alone a genocidal past a calculated attack on wholesome Australian values. Was it not "weird", he wrote, "that some Australians wanted to believe racist whites—their own fore-bears—snatched Aboriginal children from despairing mothers' arms"? (*Herald-Sun* 23/9/1999) These accusations were made, he thought, by people who took pleasure in feeling superior to ordinary, decent folk. More sinisterly, he was of the opinion that such people were using the stolen generations issue to entrench their own "status and power". (*Herald-Sun* 13/4/2000) Following Sorry Day, Andrew Bolt suggested the creation of Gratitude Day. He characterised events like Sorry Day as "cel-ebrations of guilt", where "tens of thousands" of people "mooched" around signing Sorry Books. There is, he argued, "only so much apolo-gising a person can do before they crack". (*Herald-Sun* 27/5/1998) In one of his columns Bolt suggested a national apology to the kind of people the elites despised, "those Australians who are just trying to lead a decent life—raising families, earning a wage, paying taxes, obeying the road rules, waiting patiently in queues ..." (*Herald-Sun* 15/5/2000)

In essence McGuiness and Duffy shared Bolt's sociological interpreta-tion of the elite enthusiasm for *Bringing them home*. According to McGuinness, the left-wing intelligentsia was trying to change "the moral balance of power" in Australia over the question of reconciliation and the stolen generations; trying, in a mood of deep "self-hatred", to "humili-ate" their country by calls for an apology to the Aborigines and by chat-ter about "shame and guilt". (*Sydney Morning Herald* 21/3/1998; *Sydney Morning Herald* 26/11/1998) According to Michael Duffy, the pro-Aboriginal intelligentsia were "white maggots" who were trying to "suck the blood" (sic) from the Aborigines. (*Daily Telegraph* 25/3/2000) Duffy was of the opinion that most Australians would support the idea of rec-onciliation so long as the Aborigines and their supporters would agree to "stop talking about the past". He regarded this as "a physically healthy" instinct. (*Daily Telegraph* 27/5/2000) In their obsessive concern with the past the intelligentsia was playing with fire. When Sir William Deane suggested a monument to the Aboriginal victims of the frontier massacres, Duffy pointed out that "the process of depriving us of our history is psychologically dangerous for many people". (*Daily Telegraph* 2/11/1998) He was particularly concerned at the interest of Jewish intellectuals in Aboriginal history and the links they were supposedly making between "Australian history" and "the Nazi Holocaust". "These growing links between Jewish and Aboriginal Australians", he pointed out to his *Daily Telegraph* audience, "could have a profound effect on how all Australians come to view our past, and therefore ourselves." (*Daily Telegraph* 5/1/2000) Perhaps Jewish maggots might in the end do even more psychological damage to their country than Anglo-Irish maggots like Sir Ronald Wilson and Sir William Deane.

It was clear to those involved in the right-wing campaign that not only self-hating intellectuals but also Aborigines had accepted the *Bringing them home* report. Why? On some occasions the campaigners claimed that the Aborigines who had been removed were using the myth of the stolen generations in order to disguise from themselves their own sad stories of parental neglect. "Forty-odd years of trying to make sense out of what must have felt like brutal maternal rejection", Christopher Pearson explained, "is something people from stable families can barely imagine." (*Australian Financial Review* 8/3/1999) More commonly, however, the strange phenomenon of thousands of Aborigines believing themselves to have been taken from their parents unjustly was explained by the idea that almost all were in the grip of collective hysteria and suffering from "false memory syndrome"—an opinion endorsed by Brunton, Pearson, Duffy and, of course, McGuinness.

Characteristically, Piers Akerman's explanations for Aboriginal acceptance of the basic truth of *Bringing them home* were most insulting and most extreme. Akerman doubted whether Aborigines had sufficient historical knowledge to understand complicated questions like these. When in August 2000 Cathy Freeman spoke about the removal of her grandmother and relocation to Palm Island, he suggested that the "grasp of history" of this "child–person" was "about the same level as her knowledge of her own business dealings". For Akerman the question of the Aborigines and *Bringing them home* came down to this: "Would the urban dwellers claiming Aboriginality be content with an apology if it could not legally be construed as an admission of guilt? The answer, sadly, is not likely … It's the buck, not the sentiment that counts." (*Daily Telegraph* 3/8/2000)

THE HOWARD GOVERNMENT SHOWS ITS HAND

There can be little doubt that the ministers and public servants in the Howard government responsible for Aboriginal policy watched with interest the growing political campaign against *Bringing them home*.

The Howard government came to power in March 1996 determined to overturn the regime of "political correctness" which it believed Paul Keating and the left-leaning elites in the media and the universities had imposed upon Australia. A phrase of its favourite historian, Geoffrey Blainey, about "black armband history", was ringing in its ears. From almost its first moment in office it adopted an attitude of suspicion towards the inquiry the Keating government had commissioned into the stolen generations. Every State and Territory in Australia assisted the Wilson–Dodson inquiry by the production of a detailed report into the policy and practice of Aboriginal child removal based upon a scrutiny of the archival records under its control. By contrast, under the Prime Ministership of John Howard, the Commonwealth government produced a brief, belated and largely valueless report, even though it had been responsible for Aboriginal policy in the Northern Territory between 1911 and 1978 and already had available to it the results of extensive archival investigations undertaken at the time of the first Northern Territory stolen generations test case (Kruger et al v. the

Commonwealth). When the Wilson–Dodson inquiry approached the Howard government for a small amount of additional funding, it was refused, as we have seen.

In May 1997, at the time *Bringing them home* was tabled in Federal Parliament, the tensions between the Howard government and the Wilson–Dodson inquiry were finally revealed. Howard government ministers accused the Human Rights and Equal Opportunity Commission of leaking parts of its report to the press. A journalist at the *Sydney Morning Herald* let it be known that officials of the government were orchestrating an "off the record" campaign aimed at undermining the credibility of both Mick Dodson and Sir Ronald Wilson.

The formal response of the Howard government to *Bringing them home* emerged gradually during the course of 1997. Neither the Prime Minister nor the Minister for Aboriginal Affairs, Senator Herron, denied that large numbers of Aboriginal children had in the past been removed forcibly from their mothers and families. Neither denied that this was wrong. Both offered their personal apologies to the stolen generations, whatever this might mean. Both also indicated, however, that unlike every State government the Commonwealth had no intention of supporting a federal parliamentary apology to the stolen generations. In a letter to Father Frank Brennan, Senator Herron explained the thinking thus: "The government does not support an official national apology. Such an apology could imply that present generations are in some way responsible and accountable for the actions of earlier generations, actions that were sanctioned by the laws of the time, and that were believed to be in the best interests of the children concerned." Over the coming years, the Howard government returned time and again to words like these to explain its failure to apologise to the stolen generations.

There were two distinct parts to the government's formula. According to the first part, all governments are supposed, as a matter of principle, to be incapable of apologising for the actions of their predecessors. It is impossible to believe that such an argument was sincerely held. Did the

Howard government genuinely think that it was not open to the present government of Japan to apologise because of what the wartime regimes had done to Korean "comfort women" or Australian prisoners of war? The more plausible explanation for the Howard government's unwillingness was contained in the formula's second half. Perhaps it seriously believed that because the separation of Aboriginal children from their families was lawful and undertaken by governments and missionaries whose intentions were benign, no apology to the stolen generations was due. Although after more than two years of unrelenting political pressure the Howard government was willing to allow the parliament to express its "deep and sincere regret" about past mistreatment of the Aborigines (even now forcible child removal was not explicitly mentioned), from its initial unwillingness to apologise to the stolen generations the Howard government would not be moved.

The Howard government's unwillingness to apologise determined the nature of its response to other recommendations contained in *Bringing them home*. Because it refused to consider the present generation of Australians legally or morally responsible for the mistakes of the past, it refused altogether *Bringing them home*'s recommendation for financial compensation for members of the stolen generations. Because it thought the policies of child removal had been lawful and well-intentioned, it treated almost with contempt the arguments in *Bringing them home* which suggested that in removing Aboriginal children from their families by force previous Australian governments had committed serious violations of the human rights treaties they had signed or even acts of genocide. Because, nonetheless, it accepted that the Aboriginal children who had been taken from their families had suffered serious harm it was willing to allocate modest sums to assist members of the stolen generations with psychological counselling, family reunion, cultural projects, oral histories and so on.

Despite its rejection of the most important arguments and recommendations of *Bringing them home*, there was no clear evidence in 1997 and 1998 to suggest how close the Howard government was to the anti-stolen generations campaign. On one occasion Senator Herron described the past practice of forcible child removal as "horrific". His Prime Minister described it as a "gross injustice". These crocodile tears were misleading. Beneath the political surface, something rather different was going on.

In 1996 two members of the stolen generations in the Northern Territory, Lorna Cubillo and Peter Gunner, issued writs against the Commonwealth alleging wrongful imprisonment and breaches of its statutory duty, fiduciary duty and duty of care. In order to defend itself against these charges the Commonwealth government engaged the services of a legal team headed by Douglas Meagher QC. The case was heard before Justice Maurice O'Loughlin in the Federal Court. On 1 March 1999, at Darwin, Meagher delivered his opening address on behalf of his client, the Commonwealth government. It continued for more than two days. At this moment the Howard government openly joined the anti-stolen generations campaign.

In his opening address Meagher was more concerned with the reputation of Australia than the finer points of law. In the writs issued by Cubillo and Gunner, "astonishing" and "appalling" allegations had been made against "this country". These allegations suggested that with the Aboriginal child removal policy in the Northern Territory, Australian governments had been involved in programs for the "breeding out of colour" whose purpose was the "destruction of race". With the laying of these charges, the good name of Australia, and of its leading politicians and public servants in the first two-thirds of the twentieth century, had been impugned. Meagher regarded the case before the Federal Court as an opportunity to "refute", once and for all, the mischievous allegations that had been laid.

According to Douglas Meagher the policy of Aboriginal child removal in the Northern Territory had been motivated exclusively, ever since 1911, by a concern for the welfare and educational needs of the individual Aboriginal child. Early in his address Meagher spoke of one of the first

Chief Protectors in the Northern Territory, the anthropologist Baldwin Spencer. Spencer, he claimed, was a disciple not of Charles Darwin but John Ruskin, who was known, Meagher continued, as "the father of welfare" throughout the western world. According to Meagher, Ruskin "promoted the concept of the poverty trap which could be avoided only by the removal of children from their poverty-stricken conditions". The struggle to rescue Aboriginal children from "the poverty trap" was the "underlying motivation ... for the initial removal policy".

Meagher was aware that counsel for Cubillo and Gunner intended "to place some emphasis" on the eugenics policy of a later Chief Protector, Dr Cecil Cook. Meagher argued that such emphasis was altogether misplaced. Cook was a friend of the "half-caste" not an enemy. To prove his point Meagher quoted from a memorandum Cook had written in 1931 in response to certain criticisms from the Reverend John Morley. He omitted, however, to mention that in this very memorandum Cook had written of "the incalculable future menace" the "half-caste" posed in the tropics to White Australia and to "purity of race". With friends like these ... Somewhat grudgingly Meagher conceded that on occasion Cook had written about the policy of "breeding out the colour". He assured the court, however, that this represented merely a private opinion of Dr Cook. "Where's the evidence", Meagher asked in regard to the policy of breeding out the colour, "that the [Commonwealth] government ever accepted it? It simply isn't there." As we have already seen, irrefutable archival evidence exists to show that the Federal government supported Cook's "half-caste" eugenics policy from 1932 until the end of 1938. In preparing for this case the Commonwealth spent millions of dollars on research. In the course of his opening address, moreover, Meagher quoted from the very file in which this material is contained. In claiming that the Commonwealth government never supported Dr Cook's eugenics policy for the biological assimilation of the "half-caste", what Meagher argued in court was wrong.

And not only that. Very frequently in this address Meagher showed an astonishing blindness to the racism in the policy documents he read out, often at tedious length. On one occasion Meagher quoted a memorandum of the Director of Native Affairs in the early post-war years, Frank Moy. Moy wrote: "The part-Aborigine is striving to get away from his Aboriginal ancestry. He cannot feel proud of his parents who were, in most cases, an ignorant Aboriginal woman virtually raped by a dissolute white ..." What this passage proved to Meagher was that Moy was "supportive of the half-castes". On another occasion he quoted from a document in which Moy argued that precisely because "half-caste" children "have a natural affinity to the Aborigines ... it is in their interest [that] they be removed to an institution". Meagher considered this a good example of non-racist thought. Meagher quoted Moy's admission that in inter-war Australia "half-castes" were regarded as "subhumans". He did not appear to see how Moy's remark altogether undermined his own argument that, even before the Second World War, "half-caste" children were separated from their mothers by sensitive Ruskin-inspired protectors only after consideration of their individual needs and in order to cater for their education and rescue them from the "poverty trap".

The hero of Douglas Meagher's opening address was undoubtedly the Minister for Territories under Menzies and the architect of post-war assimilation policy, Paul Hasluck. The Howard government's barrister devoted a very considerable part of his opening address to reading to the court long extracts from Hasluck's speeches and books. For him, clearly, Hasluck was still the "outstanding" man in the history of Aboriginal policy. There was nothing in his address which suggested even slight discomfort with the Hasluckian views he outlined—that it is best if the Aboriginal child is removed from its mother before the age of two; that the institutionalisation of young children does them no harm; that there is no serious difference between the process of reforming a delinquent and assimilating an Aborigine; that Aborigines must assimilate to the European world even if the price they have to pay is loss of language and culture; and that in its Aboriginal policy Australia had no alternative but to choose between one of two policies, either to segregate the Aborigines or to assimilate them to the European world. To read Meagher's opening address is to be transported back in time, to the early 1960s. The idea animating the policy of all Australian governments since the 1970s, Aboriginal self-determination, had not occurred to him.

In his opening speech to the court Meagher, in short, offered an unambiguous defence of Aboriginal child removal in assimilationist terms. In his closing submission he described the Aboriginal child removal policy as straightforwardly "meritorious". Douglas Meagher, of course, was not speaking as a private citizen, but on behalf of his client—the Commonwealth government.

It was not necessarily wrong of the Howard government to conduct a robust legal defence against the claims of Lorna Cubillo and Peter Gunner. What was wrong, however, was the decision to conduct that defence by distorting the historical record, resurrecting the assimilationist philosophy and congratulating itself on the wisdom and humanity of removing Aboriginal children of mixed descent from mother, family and world. Consider, if you will, a case where descendants of African slaves decided to sue for damages the government of the United States. No-one could regard it as wrong for the government to defend itself. Equally, no-one could think it right if, in the course of this defence, counsel for the United States government showered the institution of slavery with praise. In a case as important for the future of the relations between Aboriginal and non-Aboriginal Australians as the Cubillo–Gunner stolen generations test case, Commonwealth responsibilities ought to have extended well beyond concern for the public purse. Taxpayers are also citizens. Citizens have a right to expect from their government not only fiscal prudence but also some concern for racial justice and historical truth. With the morally indecent defence it offered of child removal policy during the course of the Cubillo–Gunner case, which was almost certainly unnecessary from the legal point of view, the Howard government became a key player in the anti-stolen generations campaign.

As the case continued there were telling signs of co-operation between anti-*Bringing them home* campaigners and Howard government officials or their legal team. One example was the appearance in the press of carefully selected verbatim extracts from the daily transcript of proceedings in the Cubillo–Gunner case, helpful to the Commonwealth side. On one occasion Frank Devine published extracts from the cross-examination of Peter Gunner concerning the question of whether or not his mother had tried to kill him at birth. (*Australian* 17/4/2000) On another occasion Michael Duffy reproduced a passage from the court transcript in which Douglas Meagher called one of the Aboriginal witnesses for Peter Gunner an outright liar, who had concocted a story about sexual abuse at St Mary's for financial gain. (*Daily Telegraph* 11/9/1999) Although in his judgment Justice O'Loughlin would find the infanticide story unproven and claims of sexual abuse at St Mary's sustained, no doubt this kind of edited extract had the desired effect in the battle for public opinion that was being waged. I could not help wondering whether Frank Devine, Michael Duffy and others were dutiful readers of the extremely voluminous daily transcripts or whether useful extracts were being sent to friendly journalists by public servants, ministerial staffers or members of the Commonwealth's legal team.

This was not the only sign of political co-operation. In June 1999 *Quadrant* published the Marsh and Howson contributions to the "rescued generations" theme. Shortly after, *Quadrant* organised a one-day conference where the argument was resumed. The after-dinner address was delivered by Senator Herron, the Minister for Aboriginal Affairs.

The following year a Senate inquiry was conducted into the adequacy of the Howard government's response to the recommendations of *Bringing them home*. The anti-stolen generations campaign had long been highly critical of the Wilson–Dodson inquiry for its failure to "call" before it the patrol officers, public servants and missionaries who had once administered the Aboriginal child removal policy. Padraic McGuinness noticed that none of these witnesses had offered to give evidence before the

Senate. On 10 June 2000 he published an article in the *Sydney Morning Herald* castigating the Howard government for its characteristic incompetence in failing to ensure that pro-removal witnesses who might give evidence to the Senate had volunteered. It is difficult to believe it a coincidence that on the very day McGuinness sent his article to the *Herald*, letters from the Office of Indigenous Affairs in the Prime Minister's Department encouraging the appearance before the Senate committee were sent to Reginald Marsh; to the former patrol officer, Les Penhall; to the former head of St Mary's, Sister Eileen Heath; and to the one Aborigine, Marjorie Harris, who was known to be grateful to the government for separating her from her family and sending her to the Retta Dixon "half-caste" Home.

In April 2000 the Howard government sent its own submission on *Bringing them home* to the Senate inquiry. Until that moment the government's attitude to Aboriginal child removal had been rather difficult to read. In Canberra the responsible ministers had described the separation policies as "tragic" and "horrific". In Darwin counsel representing the Commonwealth had described the selfsame policies as "meritorious" and praised its assimilationist foundations in glowing terms. With its Senate submission the Howard government finally came clean about its true attitude to the stolen generations.

The most interesting aspect of its submission—the one that most shocked those Australians who hoped for reconciliation—was the attempt it made to deconstruct what it regarded as the stolen generations myth. Since it was coined by Peter Read in the early 1980s, the term "stolen generations" had become for Aboriginal Australians what the term the Holocaust was for the Jews—a way of referring, in a kind of moral shorthand, to a common and collective tragedy. It now became clear, however, that the Howard government had grave misgivings about this term.

The government was, first of all, uncomfortable with the "image" the word "stolen" conjured—"of a small child snatched from the arms of his or her mother". It was convinced that in many cases the separated children were removed because they were neglected or that they had been relinquished voluntarily. Moreover, it argued against the idea that a "generation" had been removed. *Bringing them home* had claimed that from 1910 to 1970 between one in three and one in ten children had been separated from their parents. The government submission argued—convincingly in my opinion—that no good evidence existed for the upper limit and that the lower limit, taken from the 1994 ABS study, was far more sound. If "only" 10% of Aboriginal children had been removed, was not the idea of a generation or of generations absurd?

The arguments which the government used in their efforts to deconstruct the stolen generations myth were pedantic and tactless in almost equal measure. As we have seen, a large proportion of Aboriginal children separated from their parents between 1910 and 1970 were, in fact, "stolen", in the precise sense that they were removed without the need for either the consent of the parent or proof of neglect being offered to the scrutiny of a court. Even when courts and social workers were involved in separations, very many children were removed from Aboriginal parents who had neither the money nor the understanding of the legal process to resist. Nor were the government's misgivings about the idea of a "generation" or "generations" more soundly based. In ordinary language the idea of a generation is frequently used to describe the collective experience of a particular group, not necessarily the experience of all. As I was writing this essay I heard on the radio a symphony which was dedicated to the memory of the "lost generation", those young Australians who had died in the First World War. No-one would object to this phrase on the ground that not all young Australians or even a majority had been killed between 1914 and 1918.

To be informed by a government that there was no "stolen generation" because some children had been removed because of neglect or voluntarily given up, or because 10% did not constitute, according to a dictionary definition, a generation was rather like telling the Jews that there had been no Holocaust (literally a burnt sacrifice) because Hitler's victims had died by gas or gun and not by fire. Shortly after the government Senate submission was leaked to the press, I attended a meeting called by the Council for Aboriginal Reconciliation. The Aboriginal members at this meeting were angered, bewildered and hurt by the Howard government's contention that no stolen generation existed.

Beyond arithmetic and pedantry, the Senate submission proceeded down paths already familiar to readers of this essay. It repeated many of the methodological criticisms of the Wilson–Dodson inquiry pioneered by Ron Brunton; treated Colin McLeod's thin and jejune memoir as an authoritative account of removal policy; and quoted uncritically the simplistic and erroneous "half-caste as outcast" theories of Reginald Marsh. More seriously, the government submission followed Douglas Meagher and the Commonwealth's legal team in its assessment of Aboriginal child removal policy—simultaneously sentimentalising the attitude of the administrators as one of "care, concern, compassion and humanity", while altogether bleaching out of the picture the fundamental racism involved, the determination to rescue part-whites from the degradation of an Aboriginal life. Most seriously of all, as with all the contributions to the anti-stolen generations campaign, it did not even bother to discuss that evidence which revealed the racial engineering, eugenic basis of Aboriginal child removal policy and practice in both the Northern Territory and Western Australia. This evidence is, of course, at the heart of the discussion about genocide and the stolen generations.

Although the submission concluded, somewhat formulaically, that "the Howard government deeply regrets the harm caused by past policies and practices which separated indigenous families", it also flatly denied, explicitly with regard to the Northern Territory, implicitly with regard to Australia as a whole, that in the policy or practice of Aboriginal child removal any "violations of human rights" had been involved. Naturally if there had been no such violations no national apology needed to be offered, no compensation needed to be paid. Having finally revealed its position on the stolen generations, the government bunkered down until the brief storm of indignation its submission had excited died down.

The Howard government and the anti-stolen generation campaigners now waited, no doubt anxiously, for the decision of Justice O'Loughlin in the Cubillo–Gunner case. The judgment was delivered on 11 August 2000. O'Loughlin accepted that both Lorna Cubillo and Peter Gunner had suffered long-term psychological damage as a consequence of their removal and that they had experienced, during their periods of institutionalism, physical and sexual abuse. Yet he comprehensively dismissed their claims for damages on a variety of legal grounds—the prejudice to the Commonwealth's defence because of the lapse of time; the nature of the ordinance under which Cubillo and Gunner had been removed which, in the judge's opinion, did not create a vicarious liability in the Commonwealth for the actions of its Directors of Welfare or Native Affairs; and perhaps most importantly of all, the absence of crucial documentary evidence in the case of Lorna Cubillo and the presence, in the case of Peter Gunner, of several documents, including one with the thumb-print of his mother authorising her son's removal to St Mary's half-caste home. The anti-stolen generations campaigners did not disguise their pleasure at this judgment. Appearing before the Senate committee, Senator Herron now read out, for its edification, critical paragraphs from what O'Loughlin had to say. Michael Duffy captured the campaign's collective mood. "The 'stolen generation' myth is disintegrating. It has evaporated each time it has had to face serious questioning." (*Daily Telegraph* 2/9/2000)

Shortly before the judgment John Howard agreed to relaunch *Quadrant* on its return from Melbourne to Sydney. He offered to its editor, Padraic McGuinness—the general of the anti-stolen generations campaign—his highest praise. The political meaning of this was all too clear.

In order to analyse and, as it turned out, celebrate the Commonwealth's victory over Lorna Cubillo and Peter Gunner, in September 2000 *Quadrant* organised a weekend seminar with the title "Truth and Sentimentality". The opening address was delivered by none other than Douglas Meagher.

Meagher told his audience that he had hesitated when first approached by the Howard government to lead the legal team in the second stolen generations test case. In the 1960s Meagher's father, Ray, had been Chairman of the Aboriginal Welfare Board and Minister for Aboriginal Affairs under the Bolte government in Victoria. Was it not possible that if he became involved in the Cubillo–Gunner case this familial connection might affect his judgment? When he realised, though, that this case would be concerned exclusively with the Northern Territory, he agreed. Meagher informed the *Quadrant* audience that he had assumed that Aboriginal policy during the incumbency of this father could not possibly be of interest to the Wilson–Dodson inquiry—in other words that no separations of Aboriginal children from their parents had taken place in Victoria during the 1960s. For this reason he had not even bothered to read *Bringing them home* when it first appeared. After a year he read it. He was utterly appalled with what he found. He plunged into detail at once.

Bringing them home had argued that in Victoria a scheme to bring Aboriginal children from the Queensland reserves to Melbourne for the Christmas holidays, the Harold Blair Project, had a secret "strategy" for the permanent separation of Aboriginal children from their parents. Blair, an Aboriginal singer, had been an occasional guest at his father's home. Meagher "found it impossible to believe that Harold Blair would have lent his support to such a scheme; nor that my father would have done so; nor that any officer of the Queensland Aboriginal Affairs Department [sic] would have done so". How, then, had *Bringing them home* come to cast this "appalling slur"? On page ten of the report, "Mary" (witness number

214) was "recorded as saying that the people with whom she was staying whilst in Melbourne, as part of the Holiday Scheme, requested and received approval from some unidentified authority to adopt her, without reference to her parents." If this were true, Meagher conceded, there were grounds for "justifiable misgivings". But was it, in fact, true? On page sixty-six of the report, according to Meagher, circumstances altogether different were revealed, without even the courtesy of a cross-reference. "In this extract Mary says that whilst she was with the people in Melbourne her mother died and, a few sentences later, that her father died. This significantly eroded the significance of the earlier extract where it was said her adoption took place without reference to her parents." According to Meagher there was absolutely no evidence that the Harold Blair Aboriginal Children's Project was ever used to separate children from their parents. Were not such "dreadful accusations ... against the men and women who formed and implemented the policies of that era" typical of a report which, in its reliance on the memories of Aborigines, lacked the kind of "rigorous analysis" expected by people such as Douglas Meagher?

One of the members of the audience at the *Quadrant* conference was Frank Devine. On 14 September 2000 he devoted a large part of his column to Meagher's revelations about *Bringing them home*'s scandalous distortions of the evidence in the case of "Mary" and its "demonisation of good people" like Harold Blair. "I dwell on this anecdote", Devine wrote, "because it is such a sharp—almost melodramatic—example of a frail wisp of evidence being used for broad portrayal of wrongdoing." I find myself partly in agreement with Frank Devine. This anecdote is indeed highly revealing, although what it in fact reveals is the precise opposite of what he had in mind.

The first problem with the Meagher anecdote is that it is founded on a falsehood. In the extract of the evidence of "Mary", appearing on page sixty-six of *Bringing them home*, it is made crystal clear that when, at the age of seven and after her mother's death, Mary was fostered out in Melbourne, her father was still alive. "Well, I was fostered when I was 7.

I was staying with my foster parents and they rang up one day and said my mother had died and would they consider fostering me … I want to know why because my father was still alive, and he didn't die until I was 10." Not only was "Mary" fostered while her father was alive. She was also separated from her sisters and informed of her father's death by a single telephone call. In his *Quadrant* address Meagher comprehensively misstated the facts of this case.

And not only them. As we have seen, Meagher treats the claim in *Bringing them home* that the Harold Blair Project was involved in a scheme of separating Aboriginal children from their parents as a characteristically baseless and vicious slur. Once again he is wrong. The facts are much more disturbing—and interesting—than is dreamt of in the philosophy of Douglas Meagher QC.

The Harold Blair Aboriginal Children's Holiday Project—which offered Christmas holidays in Melbourne—was born in 1962. On 22 July of that year Harold Blair wrote to the superintendent at the Cherbourg Aboriginal Settlement in Queensland. He pointed out that since the visit of a troupe of Aboriginal marching girls during Moomba, which had excited great popular interest, the cast of the melodrama currently playing in Melbourne, *Uncle Tom's Cabin* (with Blair as Uncle Tom), had begun to investigate the possibility of a Christmas holiday scheme. Their scheme had captured the public imagination. Already they had received offers of assistance "some from families wanting children for holidays and others offering permanent homes either as adoptive or foster parents".

The letter continued:

> Knowing little of the legal and other problems associated with adoption of these children and provision of holidays for them so far from home, the committee has asked me to seek advice on these matters. I immediately thought of you as the man most qualified to advise me of the best means of arranging these visits *and of the possibility of, and procedure for, procuring children for fostering and adoption.* [My emphasis]

Blair's letter was passed on to the Queensland Director of Native Affairs, Cornelius O'Leary, who replied on 4 September 1962. O'Leary pointed out that recent experience showed it had "not been possible to locate parents who were prepared to offer their children for adoption". He thought that with regard to adoptions the scheme had little prospect of success. Blair was not so easily discouraged. On 5 February 1963 he and an associate, Molly Pettett of North Balwyn, visited the mothers at Cherbourg whose children had been given holidays in Melbourne. They identified four mothers who they believed might be willing to hand over their children for adoption. In March the first such handover—actually in a blaze of publicity on an afternoon television program—occurred.

While in Brisbane in February, Mrs Pettett had discussed the adoption or foster home possibility with O'Leary. He encouraged her but suggested she also make contact with the Victorian Aboriginal Welfare Board. This she apparently did. On 19 February 1963 its superintendent, Philip Felton, wrote to O'Leary outlining his misgivings in detail. "The arrangement of a short holiday is a very different matter from their permanent placement under foster home conditions." In a second letter Felton explained that "the only children" he would happily consider "for transfer interstate for legal adoption" were "infants under the age of six months, preferably of light complexion".

Felton's letters initiated a prolonged bureaucratic battle between Aboriginal Welfare in Melbourne and Native Affairs in Brisbane. O'Leary wrote to Mrs Pettett advising her once more to meet with Felton. The Queensland government, he explained, fully supported the adoption of Aboriginal children. Queensland was determined, he explained, "to have these children assimilated when white people want to take them and coloured parents wish to give them". Children were "a salient factor in Queensland's assimilation policy". On 19 April 1963 O'Leary wrote to Felton concerning adoptions and Harold Blair. On 15 May, after meeting Blair and Mrs Pettett, Felton replied:

It is evident that there is a difference of approach on this matter between this Office and Mr Blair's group and I see no possibility of our views being reconciled. The view of the group appears to be that for the sake of the children in question they should be transferred from their present hopeless environment into 'white' homes in Melbourne, where they will develop in a 'normal' way and eventually be 'assimilated' ... Their general approach is rather paternal, and they have an outmoded view of what assimilation means.

For almost three years tension existed over the fosterings taking place in connection with the Harold Blair project. On 24 January 1966 the new Queensland Director, Patrick Killoran, expressed his pleasure that some of the earlier objections to the fostering in Victoria of Queensland's Aboriginal children had dissipated. For his part he let Felton know that he had asked the Harold Blair group to maintain a greater separation between their holiday and fostering activities. Obviously between 1963 and 1966 no such separation had been observed.

The meaning of this correspondence is clear. From the moment of its inception, those who operated the Harold Blair Christmas Holiday Scheme saw it as a means by which some of the Aboriginal children might be separated permanently from their parents and assimilated into the European world. Over this question *Bringing them home*, although unaware of Phillip Felton's resistance, is essentially accurate. In his righteous indignation about *Bringing them home*'s baseless slurs on Harold Blair, Douglas Meagher proves himself both prejudiced and blind.

And not only that. On 26 September 2000 the *Australian* published a letter from Keith McEwan, in response to Frank Devine's column, which pointed out in plainest language the factual error he had made about "Mary" and *Bringing them home*. Meagher's speech was published in the November issue of *Quadrant*. Meagher's error, which had been revealed five weeks earlier, was simply allowed to stand. Apparently basic truthfulness was of little concern to those leading the anti-stolen generations campaign.

Meagher's errors with regard to Harold Blair were by no means the only misrepresentations his *Quadrant* speech contained. In defence of his father's reputation, Meagher spoke glowingly of Pastor Doug Nicholls and of his close relations with Meagher's father. He also spoke about the closing down of the Lake Tyers Aboriginal Settlement. What he somehow omitted to mention, however, was that Nicholls had resigned in 1963 from the Victorian Aborigines Welfare Board precisely because of Ray Meagher's attempt to close the Lake Tyers Settlement and to force the hundred or so Aborigines who lived there to leave. Doug Nicholls' biographer, Mavis Thorpe, explains that although he knew conditions there were bad, he also knew that if the Lake Tyers Aborigines were thrown off the reserve they would have neither the life experience nor the resources to survive. He believed that most would fall into a condition of even deeper destitution and have their children taken from them as a result. In recent years, as Nicholls would have been aware, Aboriginal children had been picked up and charged with neglect after well-publicised police raids on Aboriginal fringe camps around Mooroopna, Dimboola, Orbost and Robinvale.

In February 1963 the question of the attempted closure of Lake Tyers was debated in the Victorian Parliament. Ray Meagher offered a standard assimilationist defence of the proposed expulsion of its inhabitants. He labelled continuing the right of Aborigines to live at Lake Tyers as consistent with a policy of apartheid. In addition he asked, "Do we desire a great influx of aborigines to the territory?" Ray Meagher had previously argued that unless children were given "the opportunity to acclimatise to the European type of society in which we are going to ask them to live, they will never make the grade." Moreover, as the Deputy Leader of the Opposition, Clyde Holding, pointed out, the Melbourne *Herald* had recently quoted Ray Meagher's opinion that "a backward dark person is merely a 'depressed' white and can be adapted to white living if caught early enough." Aboriginality here sounded like a disease.

In the Victoria of Henry Bolte and Ray Meagher the question of

Aboriginal child removal remained, from many different angles, very much alive. This is what Douglas Meagher cannot or will not see. For him the assimilationist attitudes and polices are, quite simply, beyond question and above reproach. For him the Commonwealth's defence in the Cubillo–Gunner case seems to have been more than just an ordinary brief. It was part of a mission to vindicate the assimilation era and his father's good name. In everything he said about the issue of the stolen generations Douglas Meagher proved himself incapable of seeing the injustice done to the Aborigines but highly sensitive to the supposed injustice inflicted by the Wilson–Dodson inquiry on the reputations of the missionaries, patrol officers, public servants, politicians and even Prime Ministers involved in child removal policy or practice.

I do not wish to be misunderstood here. Although his tone is invariably one of wounded, patriotic bombast, nevertheless Meagher has put his finger on an issue which needs to be seriously discussed.

No-one can undertake a study of those involved in Aboriginal child removal policy without encountering figures exemplifying every moral type—from brutal sadists to selfless saints. Equally, no-one can fail to discover, even among the kindest of human beings involved in the removal process, ways of thinking that are disfigured by the all-pervasive racism of the times. One of the women involved in Aboriginal child removal, who was deeply admired by all who knew her, was Sister Kate, the founder of the Perth "quarter-caste" home given her name. On one occasion she wrote to the Chief Protector of Aborigines in Western Australia, A. O. Neville, like this: "We should of course like to have the poorest and most neglected children, not those who have mothers who love and care for them, but those who are most unwanted to the State. But that we must leave to you." Another greatly admired woman involved in child separation was the first superintendent of St Mary's Hostel in post-war Alice Springs, Sister Eileen Heath. Once, in administrative mode, she wrote: "The separation of the full blood and the half-caste is desirable. It is quite obvious that if they are allowed to continue to mix, assimilation will be retarded." Under the influence, then, of prevailing racist ways of thought from which they could not emancipate themselves, Sister Kate was willing to allow babies to be separated from mothers who loved and cared for them, while Sister Eileen Heath was keen to keep "half-caste" children segregated from "full bloods".

To treat, as Douglas Meagher does, the analysis of *Bringing them home* as a kind of personal attack on those involved in the removal process, is to close one's eyes to what is probably the most important lesson it has to teach—namely how almost no-one was able to see through the kind of racism which could make it seem that tearing Aboriginal children from their mothers and communities was a natural, even noble, act.

DENIALISM REACHES THE FRONTIER

Only one other speech at *Quadrant*'s September 2000 seminar captured some public interest—Keith Windschuttle's summary of a 35,000 word article he called "The Myths of Frontier Violence". From one point of view Windschuttle's appearance at the "Truth and Sentimentality" seminar was odd. His interest was not in the stolen generations but in the killings of Aborigines on the colonial frontier. From another point of view, however, his appearance at this gathering made complete sense. An ideological logic was by now determining the direction of the anti-*Bringing them home* campaign. According to this logic, just as the stories of forcible Aboriginal child removal had been exaggerated or concocted altogether, so too had the stories of frontier massacre. With the serialisation of Windschuttle's article over three issues, *Quadrant* moved from historical denialism with regard to the stolen generations to denialism of a more general and sinister kind.

From the biographical point of view, Keith Windschuttle's involvement at the centre of historical denialism in Australia is rather strange. Once a radical leftist and an academic with an interest in capitalism and the media, during the early 1990s he began to move, rather rapidly, to the right. In 1994 Windschuttle achieved some success with a polemic attacking deconstructionist and postmodernist trends called *The Killing of History*, which was championed by the group associated with the starchily conservative American cultural journal *New Criterion*. Rescued from obscurity and reborn as an ersatz New York neo-conservative, in the late 1990s Keith Windschuttle—a sociologist of the media who had shown no previous interest in Aborigines—changed the focus of his scholarly interest from the killing of history to the history of killing in his native land. "The Myths of Frontier Massacres" was the result.

According to the argument of Windschuttle's "Myths", the stories of massacres of Aborigines in colonial Australia have been either exaggerated or manufactured, originally by neurotic Christian missionaries searching for souls and careers, much later by ideologically-driven twentieth-century leftist historians intent upon denying the legitimacy of the British settlement and denigrating Australia's good name.

Windschuttle attempted to prove his general claim by a rather curious method—the examination of the four specific massacres mentioned by the expatriate journalist Phillip Knightley in his recent popular profile, *Australia: A Biography of a Nation*. The first of these massacres is the Battle of Pinjara, which occurred near Perth in 1834. At Pinjara between ten and thirty Aborigines or more were shot dead by a party of twenty-five British troops and settlers in reprisal for an earlier Aboriginal killing of a soldier. Traditionally Pinjara has been interpreted as a punitive expedition—an attempt to pre-empt future Aboriginal violence by the spreading of a general fear. Windschuttle interprets it rather as a "lawful and morally justifiable" action which is, however, "now used by historians to question the legitimacy of the British occupation of the Australian continent and of its commitment to the rule of law and civilised values". One of the first historians to describe the Battle of Pinjara as a punitive expedition was Paul Hasluck. In *Black Australians* (1942) he wrote of Pinjara: "It is impossible to find any purpose for bringing on the 'battle' except punishment ... The 'battle' was regarded by the settlers as punishment and generally approved as such, and in similar stages of conflict in other parts of the State, it was referred to as a successful operation." Hasluck is not usually thought of as someone trying to white-ant British civilisation in Australia.

Windschuttle's description of a second famous massacre, Waterloo Creek, is, if anything, odder still. At Waterloo Creek in New South Wales in 1837, a very large number of Aborigines—how many exactly will never be known—were killed, again by a party of British troops, this time in reprisal for the killing of five white stockmen in recent years. The Christian missionary Lancelot Threkeld was outraged by what had occurred. He spoke of the deaths of 120 Aborigines or more. In a subsequent official investigation one member of the party admitted to a death toll of forty or fifty. Two others, however, claimed that only four or five Aborigines had been killed. Without even any serious discussion of the likelihood of an attempted cover-up, Windschuttle, with a completely straight face, accepts as reasonable the figure of four or five, dismisses as false the admission of forty or fifty deaths, and treats the Reverend Threkeld as a crank pursuing a Christian separatist agenda of his own. No doubt the language Windschuttle uses to analyse the Waterloo Creek massacre would appeal to his *New Criterion* friends. He shows no scepticism about the official description—a notorious frontier euphemism—of one Aboriginal casualty as having been "shot while trying to escape". He has no difficulty in describing a terrible punitive expedition mounted against desperate Aborigines driven from their ancestral lands as "a legitimate police operation to apprehend people reasonably suspected of murder".

In his "Myths" Windschuttle skips over the ninety years that separated the Battle of Pinjara and Waterloo Creek in the 1830s from the massacres at Coniston Station in the Northern Territory and at Forrest River in Western Australia in the 1920s. In regard to Coniston, Windschuttle acknowledges that a massacre of Aborigines occurred. In regard to Forrest River, however, he accepts the revisionist thesis of the journalist Rod Moran, who argued in *Massacre Myth* that no killings took place, and rejects as valueless the findings of a contemporary Royal Commission, the book of a seasoned historian, Neville Green, and the oral history accounts of the Forrest River massacres repeated over the decades by the local Aborigines. The argument between Moran and Green will be settled by the normal processes of historical argument. Yet surely even Windschuttle must understand that in the unlikely event that Moran's version of Forrest River is shown by evidence and logic to be the more plausible account, this tells us nothing whatsoever about the hundreds of well-documented cases of Aboriginal killings in small numbers or large, that took place on the colonial frontier between the 1830s and the 1920s in Western Victoria, Gippsland, northern New South Wales, the north of Western Australia, Central Australia and the Northern Territory.

Having concluded to his satisfaction that the stories of frontier massacres are myths, by the risible method of examining only the cases mentioned by Phillip Knightley and thereby overlooking ninety crucial years, Windschuttle then embarks upon an attempt to demonstrate what he calls the "fabrication" by Australian historians of the Aboriginal death toll. Used in this context fabrication is a very serious charge. It involves an accusation of a deliberate, politically motivated lie.

Assessing the number of Aboriginal frontier killings is a genuinely daunting research task. In colonial Australia, Aborigines were British subjects who could not lawfully be killed with impunity. They were in fact killed in large numbers nevertheless—by troops, settlers and the native police. Because of the discrepancy between the legal situation and what was happening on the ground, many of these deaths were never officially recorded. Moreover, especially in the remoter regions of northern Australia in the second half of the nineteenth century, a kind of conspiracy of silence prevailed with regard to particular incidents, even though frontier killings were common knowledge,. Because of this conspiracy of silence and the gaps in the official records, no-one knows, or will ever know, exactly how many Aborigines were killed on the colonial frontier.

Despite these difficulties, and despite the fact that scholarship with regard to frontier killings was still in its infancy, during the 1980s two historians tried to estimate the total number of such deaths. In 1981, in *The Other Side of the Frontier*, Henry Reynolds added the figures of earlier studies—both State-wide and local—and extrapolated from these to the country as a whole. On the basis of the earlier estimates and his extrapolation, Reynolds guessed, conservatively he thought, that perhaps 20,000 Aborigines might have been killed on the colonial frontier. In 1988 Richard Broome came to the same conclusion by a different route. European or Chinese deaths at Aboriginal hands were far more accurately recorded than Aboriginal deaths at European hands. Earlier research showed that 2,000 such deaths had occurred at most. Having surveyed estimates of ratios of Aboriginal to non-Aboriginal deaths in different parts of Australia, he concluded that a national average of ten to one was realistic and therefore also arrived at a total of 20,000 Aboriginal killings at the frontier.

Both these studies made the manner in which they arrived at their conclusions clear. Neither suggested that their conclusions were more than educated guesses which might have to be raised upwards or downwards in the light of more detailed and accurate studies that might subsequently be made. Insofar as either had a political intention, it was to counter not right-wing denialism but some of the wilder exaggerations of the number of Aboriginal frontier deaths which were beginning to appear in the radical 1980s. Even conservative scholars at first recognised that the Reynolds–Broome estimate was realistic and moderate. In 1993 Geoffrey Blainey, in *Quadrant's* Latham Lecture, identified and disapproved of what he regarded as the unduly tragic interpretation of Aboriginal dispossession which had taken hold among Australian historians. He christened this interpretation "the black-armband view". In the same lecture, however, he accepted that there had been 20,000 killings of Aborigines on the colonial frontier. Blainey is not usually regarded as a fellow traveller of the ideological left.

Unlike Blainey, Windschuttle is outraged at the Reynolds figure of 20,000 frontier killings. He had expected, he tells us, to find "a list or tabulation of the number of Aborigines who had been observed, or at least reported, killed during the nineteenth or early twentieth centuries". But no such list or tabulation could be found, beyond a few unidentified regional studies which showed, he claims, that "mass killings of Aborigines were rare and isolated phenomena". The absence of such a list does not lead Windschuttle, as one might imagine, to agnosticism with regard to the number of Aboriginal frontier killings. Although he has undertaken no research of his own on Aboriginal history (or on anything else), Windschuttle somehow knows with complete certainty that the figure of 20,000 is a vast exaggeration and "inherently implausible".

How, then, does Windschuttle know something unknown to historians of Aboriginal Australia, from Geoffrey Blainey on the right to Henry Reynolds on the left? The answer to this question, when it finally arrives, is disarming in its simplicity. The British colonies in Australia were "civilised societies governed by both morality and laws that forbade the killing of the innocent". For almost everyone in a society such as this, the power of the Christian ethic was sufficient to prevent the killing of Aborigines, even in the struggles for land and security at the frontier. Even those without a Christian conscience were inhibited by the power of the idea of the rule of law. To kill an Aborigine was to commit a murder. On the colonial frontier "there was always someone likely to report" incidents where Aborigines were killed without lawful cause. The penalty for murder in colonial Australia, Windschuttle reminds us, was death. In 1838, after the Myall Creek massacre, seven murderers of Aborigines were hanged. The Myall Creek gallows cast their shadow over the British colonies in Australia for the next 100 years. It is by this process of argument that the "inherent" implausibility of frontier massacres is revealed.

Only someone almost entirely ignorant of Aboriginal history could write nonsense of such a kind. Let us examine Windschuttle's claims, briefly, one by one.

Those who are inclined to accept Windschuttle's claim that recent regional studies show that the killings of Aborigines were "isolated" and "rare" events ought to examine the work of two scholars, Richard Kimber and Ian Clark. In the journal *Genocide Perspectives* (1997), on the basis of an unrivalled mastery of the documentary sources, Kimber reveals the existence of a huge discrepancy between the official records and unofficial reports of Aboriginal killings in Central Australia, and shows that of the approximately 4,500 Aborigines who lived in Central Australia at the time of the arrival of British settlers in 1860, by 1895 no fewer than 650 had been hunted down and shot. Ian Clark's study *Scars in the Landscape* (1995) is no less impressive and no less meticulous. Clark pieces together, from all the available documentary sources, evidence of 107 massacre sites in Western Victoria. These sites, dating mainly from the 1840s, range from sites of single killings to killings of small numbers to large-scale slaughters of between twenty or forty Aborigines and in one case possibly even more. By taking the lower estimate in Clark's tabulations, in those cases where precise numbers of the dead are recorded in the documentary evidence, 409 killings are revealed. By adding to this figure conservative approximations in those cases where the contemporary sources do not give an exact number but refer to "dozens of deaths" or to the deaths of "all but two of the clan", we arrive at a total of some 500 Aborigines killed by Europeans in Western Victoria.

Windschuttle's claim that recent regional studies undermine the estimates of Henry Reynolds and Richard Broome is simply false. Kimber's study suggests that within a period of thirty-five years nearly 15% of the number of Aborigines living in Central Australia at the time of the arrival of the British had been killed. Clark's figures suggest that if Western Victoria was typical of Victoria as a whole—and we already know that in Gippsland between 250 and 350 killings occurred—approximately one thousand Aborigines in the colony of Victoria were killed. According to the pioneering demographic work of Radcliffe-Brown, at the time of the British arrival between 3% and 4% of Australia's 300,000 Aborigines lived in Victoria. The tabulations found in Kimber and Clark are thus consistent with, although of course they do not prove, a global figure of Aboriginal frontier deaths higher than the 20,000 estimate of Henry Reynolds and Richard Broome.

If anything, Windschuttle's belief that Christian consciences or fear of legal reprisal prevented the widespread killing of Aborigines on the colonial frontier is even more wrongheaded.

Anyone who wishes to understand how easily the Christian consciences of the nineteenth-century settlers succumbed to racial hatred and genocidal fantasies about the extermination of the Aborigines, or how readily the young men took to "nigger hunts", should read the relevant chapters of Henry Reynolds' remarkable book *Frontier*. In 1883, to take only one example, the colonial civil servant Sir Arthur Gordon wrote to the great British Liberal William Gladstone about the State of Queensland. He had, he said, "heard men of culture and refinement, of the greatest humanity and kindness to their fellow whites, and who when you meet them at home you would pronounce to be incapable of such deeds, talk, not only of the *wholesale* butchery … but of the *individual* murder of natives, exactly as they would talk of a day's sport, or of having had to kill some troublesome animal."

In order to understand what racial arrogance and material greed could do to Christian consciences on the frontier, perhaps an even more illuminating guide than Reynolds is Howard Fysh's biography of the Queensland pioneer Alexander Kennedy, *Taming of the North*, in which the long and bloody task of subduing "the savage Kalkadoons" and driving them from their lands is described with the greatest candour and without a twinge of bad conscience. Those who the colonists would destroy they first dehumanised. In Fysh's work the "buck" is a cunning and treacherous cannibal, with a preference for bland Chinese meat over salty Europeans. Their "gins" and "piccaninnies" are of so base a human type that after battle, we are told, they may be seen feasting on the decomposing flesh of dead warriors. Henry Reynolds has observed that Australia in the 1930s was a more profoundly racist society than it had been a hundred years before. Fysh's work bears this out. It is instructive and shocking to learn that his work was published less than seventy years ago.

Fysh's work should also be read by those who think that fear of detection and legal reprisal prevented Aboriginal killings on the frontier. On one occasion Alexander Kennedy rode to Brisbane to speak to the Commissioner of Police about the need for action against the Aborigines. Inside the government office, the Commissioner warned: "Kennedy, if you touch one of those blacks we shall have you arrested." Kennedy left in disgust. The Commissioner caught up with him on the street outside. "Look here," he said, "I could not tell you what to do in there. We shall do what we can to increase the number of police patrols in the bad area; meanwhile, if you have trouble, you know what to do." Indeed, he did.

Fysh describes in some detail the work of the most important State instrumentality for the killing of Aborigines, the Queensland Native Police, which at its height employed 250 Europeans and deracinated Aborigines, and absorbed 6% of the colony's entire budget. The work of the Native Police was to protect settlers and their livestock from attack and to "disperse" the Aborigines. Dispersal was a well-known euphemism for killing. Far from the fear of legal reprisal preventing the large-scale killing of Aborigines, reprisal killing of Aborigines was, at certain times in Queensland and elsewhere in Central Australia and the north, the business of the state. Concerning the work of the Queensland Native Police, Windschuttle, astonishingly, says not a word.

Although from time to time in colonial Australia investigations into Aboriginal killings were undertaken and, less frequently, suspects brought to trial, in the entire century following the Myall Creek hangings, at least so far as I am aware, not one British settler, soldier or policeman was found guilty of the murder of an Aborigine. As unpunished killings continued, the shadow cast by the gallows of Myall Creek became ever fainter with the passing of the years. To deny now that large numbers of such killings ever took place is not merely absurd. It is to join the old conspiracy of silence and to deepen the original offence.

WHY?

I would ask readers of this essay at this point to cast their minds back to the stories of Walter, Margaret Tucker, Lorna Cubillo and Malcolm Smith and to consider a simple question: Why has so much energy been expended in the attempt to deny—in these cases and among the 20,000 or 25,000 cases of Aboriginal child removal which were carried out between 1900 and 1970—that a really terrible injustice occurred?

Individual motives, of course, differ. Some of the anti-*Bringing them home* campaigners are now too old or proud to reflect on the cruelty of practices in which they were personally involved. Some hanker for a return to the good old days of assimilation when Aborigines were instructed by Europeans on how they were to live. Some are loyal sons who wish to vindicate the memories of their fathers. Some are former leftists who are so obsessed by the conduct of ideological combat against their former friends that they have come to believe that truth is simply the opposite of what they once believed. Some are general pur-pose right-wingers who hunt in packs and can be relied upon to agree with whatever their political friends believe. And some have so little capacity for empathy that they genuinely cannot imagine the harm inflicted on a child taken from the warmth of a family to a loveless insti-tution where their skin colour is regarded as a cause for shame, or what depth of grief and bitterness and powerlessness is experienced by moth-ers and families who are robbed of their children by welfare workers and police.

Yet while all these explanations help us to understand the motivations of the anti-*Bringing them home* campaigners, none takes us to the campaign's heart. The tense debate over the stolen generations and the attack on the credibility of *Bringing them home* is, in my opinion, part of a larger culture war—over the meaning of Aboriginal dispossession.

Ever since the early 1970s Australians have been struggling to come to terms with the crimes committed during the settlement of their country and with the ways in which the Aborigines were treated by governments and society after the dispossession was complete.

At the time of the British arrival in 1788 there were, according to different demographic estimates, somewhere between 300,000 and 1,000,000 Aborigines living in Australia. By the 1920s, according to censuses undertaken by authorities, about 70,000 "full bloods" and "half-castes" survived. Many had succumbed to previously unknown diseases or died from malnutrition. Many, unable to cope with removal from their lands and the destruction of their world, had lost the desire to procreate. Some, on the frontier, had been shot. It is true that the tragedy which befell the Australian Aborigines was inevitable. It is inconceivable, during the age of European expansionism and racial arrogance, that Australia would remain uncolonised or, when colonised, that its indigenous people would be treated with respect. It is possible, although by no means self-evident, that the Aborigines might have suffered even more harshly if Australia had been settled by Spaniards or French rather than the British. One thing, however, is certain. During the long course of the dispossession the Aborigines were the victims of an unspeakable crime.

After the dispossession injustices did not end. Racial condescension was almost universal—captured, for example, in the insulting or comical names settlers unself-consciously gave the Aborigines and in the zoological terminology favoured by the administrators—"full bloods", "half-castes", "crossbreeds", "quadroons", "octoroons" and so on. In some parts of Australia, Aborigines were driven into penitentiary-style reserves, like Palm Island in Queensland or Moore River in Western Australia. In other parts Aborigines worked on cattle stations or in the fishing industry in return for rations but no wages. In the outback the sexual misuse of women, kidnapping of children, arbitrary arrests for cattle theft, use of neck chains to bring prisoners and witnesses to court, farcical trials and very long sentences in appalling prison conditions were all routine. Readers who doubt any of this ought to turn to the report of the Roth

Royal Commission of 1904 into the condition of the natives of the north of Western Australia.

Even in the more civilised south, injustices were commonplace. Aborigines were frequently driven away from the outskirts of the country towns where they tried to settle. Unless they were granted a "certificate of exemption" from their Aboriginality, before the Second World War even the most intimate and vital details of their lives—like whom they might marry or where they might live—were controlled by government officials to an astonishing degree. Frequently Aboriginal children were refused permission to attend government schools on the grounds that they were dirty or sexually precocious or suffering from disease. Very frequently, as we have seen, Aboriginal children were simply taken away, under one pretext or another.

Of all the questions concerning the injustices experienced by the Aborigines after the dispossession, Aboriginal child removal—perhaps because it concerned a violation universally understood, the separation of mother and child—was the one which most deeply captured the national imagination. After the publication of Bringing them home many Australians were astonished to discover what had happened so recently in their country's history and what they had previously failed to understand or even to see. This story had the power to change forever the way they saw their country's history.

Considerable numbers of Australians were not affected in a similar way. They regarded Aborigines as "a pretty incompetent lot". They were bored or irritated by the amount of attention Aborigines received. Their scepticism about the injustice done to the stolen generations, which was reflected in the anti-Bringing them home campaign, was the most important cultural expression of a growing atmosphere of right-wing and populist resistance to discussions of historical injustice and the Aborigines. One symptom of this mood was the emergence of a political force in country Australia known as Hansonism. Another symptom was the profound ambivalence of the Howard government when it came to questions of justice, Australian history and the Aborigines. Yet another symptom of this new mood was the crystallisation around *Quadrant*, the present Prime Minister's favourite magazine, of an Australian version of historical denialism with regard to what the present Governor-General once called our legacy of unutterable shame.

SOURCES

In order to help readers check the accuracy of factual claims made in this essay, sources are given below. The page numbers indicate where the arguments appear. Only the sources of information not identified in the text of the essay have been included here. I am grateful to Dr Heidi Zogbaum for her assistance in locating some of the sources for this essay.

1–3 Lowitja O'Donoghue has told her story briefly in the foreword to Rowena MacDonald, *Between Two Worlds*, IAD Press, Alice Springs, 1995, pp. vii–viii.

4 Proceedings at the conference and Robert Tickner's address can be found in *The Long Road Home: The Going Home Conference, 3rd October 1994*.

7–10 The story of Walter is contained in a file held in the Queensland State Archives, A/58751.

10–12 The Annual Report of the NSW Board for the Protection of Aborigines for the Year 1911 is printed in the parliamentary papers of the Legislative Assembly, 1912. McGarry's comments are from the debate of 27 January 1915 in the NSW Legislative Assembly, p. 1953. The Board's complaint about the difficulty of proving neglect is quoted in Heather Goodall, *Invasion to Embassy: Land in Aboriginal Politics in New South Wales, 1770–1972*, Allen & Unwin in association with Black Books, Sydney, 1996, pp. 120–1.

13–15 Margaret Tucker's story is found in her memoir, *If Everyone Cared*, Ure Smith, Sydney, 1977.

15–21 A fair-minded summary of the evidence presented in the case of

Lorna Cubillo against the Commonwealth can be found in the detailed judgment of Justice Maurice O'Loughlin of the Federal Court of 11 August 2000, paras 6–11 and 363–736.

21–24 The story of Malcolm Smith is told in J. H. Wootten, *Report of the Inquiry into the Death of Malcolm Charles Smith*, Royal Commission into Aboriginal Deaths in Custody, Australian Government Publishing Service, Canberra, 1989.

24–27 *Bringing them home*'s discussion of the number of removals is on pp. 36–37 of the report. Peter Read's discussion is in *a rape of the soul so profound*, Allen & Unwin, Sydney, 1999, pp. 25–33. The table on indigenous child separations is found on p. 7 of the *National Aboriginal and Torres Strait Islander Survey 1994: Detailed Findings*, ABS, Canberra, 1994.

31–42 Ron Brunton's *Betraying the Victims* was published as an IPA Backgrounder in February 1998.

39　　　Lothar Gall's memorandum on sterilising the Queensland "half-castes" can be found in Queensland State Archives A/8725 1859–1934.

39　　　A. O. Neville's statement to the Brisbane *Telegraph* is in *Bringing them home*, p. 30. His statement about the end of the Aboriginal people is in *Aboriginal Welfare: Initial Conference of Commonwealth and State Aboriginal Authorities*, Canberra, 1937, p. 11.

41　　　Raimond Gaita's "Genocide and the Stolen Generations" can be found in *A Common Humanity: Thinking about Love & Truth & Justice*, Text Publishing, Melbourne, 1999, pp. 131–155. My own essay "The Stolen Generations" can be found in *The Way We Live Now*, Text Publishing, Melbourne 1998, pp. 15–41. Both appeared first in *Quadrant* before the publication of *Betraying the Victims*.

42–44 The interviews with Gordon Sweeney (TS 337), Ted Evans (TS 4646) and Reginald McCaffrey (TS 85) were conducted between 1980 and 1984. All were part of the oral history project of the Northern Territory Archives Service, NTRS 226.

44   Jeremy Long's article appears in *Oceania*, 37, 1967, pp. 186–201. His later comments regarding the removal policy are found in *The Go-Betweens: Patrol Officers in Aboriginal Affairs Administration in the Northern Territory 1936–1974*, North Australia Research Unit, Australian National University, 1992.

45–47 Colin Macleod's memoir, *Patrol in the Dreamtime*, was published by Mandarin in 1997. He was cross-examined in the case of Cubillo and Gunner v. the Commonwealth on 17 November 1999. He discussed his relations with Aborigines after his time as a patrol officer in the interview he gave to the "Bringing Them Home Oral History Project" conducted by the Oral History Section of the National Library of Australia.

47   *Patrol in the Dreamtime* was quoted extensively in the Government submission to the Senate inquiry into the implementation of *Bringing them home*. Senator Herron told the *Senate* on 26 May 1999 that he had read *Patrol in the Dreamtime* and been influenced by it. In a private communication I was informed that John Howard had invited Colin Macleod to Canberra to discuss Aboriginal child removal.

47–51 Reginald Marsh's article appeared in *Quadrant* in June 1999. I interviewed Marsh for the "Bringing Them Home Oral History Project" conducted by the Oral History Section of the National Library on 17 February 2000. He said that the first time he worked in the Northern Territory was 1954. McGuinness referred to Marsh's supposed role in the movement of Charles Perkins from Alice Springs to Adelaide in *Quadrant* in November 1999 and in a number of newspaper columns.

50 Professor Kenneth Maddocks's "Anthropological Report on Lorna Cubillo and Peter Gunner v. Commonwealth" prepared for the Australian Government Solicitor is dated 13 February 1999. The reference to Elkin is on p. 81, to Diane Bell on p. 46 and to Maddocks's own field work on p. 53. The passage from Bill Harney is quoted in the daily transcript of proceedings in the case of Lorna Cubillo and Peter Gunner v. the Commonwealth, 8 November 1999.

51–57 Peter Howson's relations with Nugget Coombs can be followed in *The Howson Diaries*, Penguin, Ringwood, 1984 and in Tim Rowse's *Obliged To Be Difficult: Nugget Coombs' Legacy in Indigenous Affairs*, Cambridge University Press, Melbourne, 2000. Howson's preface was to Geoffrey Partington, *Hasluck versus Coombs:White Politics and Australia's Aborigines*, Quakers Hill Press, Sydney, 1996. "Rescued from the Rabbit Burrow" appeared in *Quadrant* in June 1999. Des Moore forwarded Peter Howson's submission to the Senate Committee on 1 June 2000. It can be found at http://www.aph.gov.au/senate/committee/submissions/lc_stolen.ht.

57 The claim that Les Murray is a political friend of Mick and Patrick Dodson is found in Peter Alexander *Les Murray: A Life in Progress*, Oxford University Press, Melbourne, 2000, p. 284. The letter from Murray to me is in my possession.

62–64 An account of the poisonings on Dr James Kilgour's station near Port Fairy can be found in Ian Clark, *Scars in the Landscape:A Register of Massacre Sites in Western Victoria, 1803–1859*, Australian Institute of Aboriginal and Torres Strait Islander Studies, Canberra, 1995, pp. 43–5. The Kangaroo Creek poisoning is discussed in Jane Lydon, "'no moral doubt ...': Aboriginal evidence and the Kangaroo Creek poisoning, 1847–1849", *Aboriginal History*, no. 20, 1996, pp. 151–165. Raymond Evans has a brief account of poisonings on the colonial frontier in Queensland in Raymond Evans et al. (eds), *Exclusion, Exploitation and Extermination: Race*

Relations in Colonial Queensland, Australia and New Zealand Book Company, Sydney, 1975, pp. 49–50.

64–65 The critical file concerning Commonwealth government support for the policy of "breeding out the colour" of the "half-castes" is held by the Australian Archives at Canberra, AA ACT A659/1 40/1/408.

69–70 Les Penhall spoke about the closure of the army camps near Phillip Creek at the end of the war in the interview he gave to the "Bringing Them Home Oral History Project" conducted by the Oral History Section of the National Library of Australia.

74–75 Sir Ronald Wilson spoke of the difficulties with the Howard government, including its refusal of additional funds, at a hearing of the Legal and Constitutional References Committee of the Senate of 4 September 2000, pp. 752–3.

76–77 Senator Herron described the practice of Aboriginal child removal as "horrific" in the *Senate* on 8 October 1996. In answer to a question concerning the stolen generations, John Howard spoke about the "gross injustices" practised against indigenous Australians in the past, *House of Representatives*, 5 April 2000.

77–80 Douglas Meagher's opening address to the Federal Court in the case of Lorna Cubillo and Peter Gunner v. the Commonwealth can be read in the daily transcript of proceedings, 1–3 March 1999.

78   Dr Cook's reply to the Reverend John Morley can be found in Australian Archives ACT AA A1/1 36/6595.

80   Douglas Meagher described the child removal policy of the Commonwealth as "meritorious" in the course of his final remarks to the court in the Cubillo–Gunner case, daily transcript of proceedings, 21 February 2000 p. 6496.

81–2   Senator Herron was questioned about the letter sent by a senior officer of his Department, Russ Street, to Les Penhall, Sister Eileen Heath, Marjorie Harris and others inviting them to give evidence before the Legal and Constitutional Committee of the Senate. The letter sent to Marjorie Harris was dated 9 June 2000, the same day McGuinness wrote his column for the *Sydney Morning Herald*. Senate, Legal and Constitutional References Committee, 18 August 2000, pp. 643–7.

85   John Howard's speech on the return of *Quadrant* from Melbourne to Sydney was published in *Quadrant* in September 2000, pp. 2–3.

86–90 The material on the Harold Blair holiday scheme is found in the Queensland State Archives, 505/1 IA/584 nos. 1–3. Philip Felton discusses his misgivings about the project in his interview with the "Bringing Them Home Oral History Project" conducted by the Oral History Section of the National Library of Australia.

91   For an account of Ray Meagher's attempt to close down the Lake Tyers settlement, see Mavis Thorpe Clark, *Pastor Doug: The Story of an Aboriginal Leader*, Lansdowne Press, Melbourne, 1965, ch. 24. The debate on its closure is in Victorian Legislative Assembly Debates, 30 April 1963, pp. 3169–3188.

91–2   Philip Felton discusses the police raids on Aboriginal camps and the removal of children which took place in Victoria in the 1950s and early 1960s in the interview he gave to the "Bringing Them Home Oral History Project" conducted by the Oral History Section of the National Library of Australia.

92–93 Sister Kate's letter is quoted in Pat Jacobs, *Mister Neville*, Fremantle Arts Centre Press, Fremantle, 1990, p. 218. Sister Eileen Heath's views on the need to segregate "half-caste" and "full blood" children were quoted by Douglas Meagher in the course of his opening address to the court in the case of Cubillo and Gunner v. the Commonwealth, 1–3 March 1999.

93–101 Keith Windschuttle's "The Myths of Frontier Massacres in Australian History" appeared in three issues of *Quadrant*, October–December 2000, vol. xliv, numbers 10–12.

96–97 Henry Reynolds's estimate of Aboriginal frontier deaths comes from *The Other Side of the Frontier: Aboriginal Resistance to the European Invasion of Australia*, Pelican Books, Melbourne, 1982, pp. 121–5. Richard Broome's estimate of Aboriginal frontier deaths is found in M. McKernan & M. Browne, *Australia: Two Centuries of War and Peace*, Australian War Memorial in association with Allen & Unwin Australia, Canberra, 1998, pp. 92–120.

99 Professor W. R. Radcliffe-Brown's estimate of 300,000 Aborigines and 11,500 in Victoria can be found in *Official Year Book of the Commonwealth of Australia*, 23, Government Printer, Melbourne, 1930, pp. 687–96.

100 The extract from the letter Sir Arthur Gordon wrote to Gladstone is found in Henry Reynolds, *Frontier: Aborigines, Settlers and Land*, Allen & Unwin, Sydney, 1987, pp. 51–2.

100–1 Hudson Fysh, *Taming the North*, Angus & Robertson, Sydney and London, 1933, enlarged and revised, 1950.

101 The figure of 6% comes from Noel Loos, *Invasion and Resistance*,

Australian National University Press, Canberra, 1982, p. 25. The maximum of 250 troops is from Raymond Evans et al. (eds), *Exclusion, Exploitation and Extermination: Race Relations in Colonial Queensland*, Australia and New Zealand Book Company, Sydney, 1975, p. 56.

103–4 Dr Walter Roth's "Commission on the Condition of the Natives" was published in the Votes and Proceedings, Western Australia, 1905.

105   According to Nicholas Rothwell in the *Australian* of 22 July 2000, John Howard now reads *Quadrant* "religiously".